THE CORPORATE HERO'S JOURNEY

Impact intrapreneurs at some of the most powerful organizations in the world are designing new, more sustainable businesses from within. They put their values to work and transform their corporations into a force for good. In a corporate world that still largely prioritizes profit above all else, these people shine a light on how to balance profit with impact, and the inspirational stories captured in this book guide leaders and managers to do the same.

The lack of purpose beyond profit is causing millions of people to question their work and even to leave the corporate world altogether. Companies are struggling with recruitment and retention, as people seek a greater sense of purpose. For many, this would mean finding a way to use their work as a platform for positive social and environmental impact. This book will inspire this change for leaders seeking a different and better way forward. Structured around the stages of Joseph Campbell's hero's journey – upon which Star Wars was based – this book combines the philosophy of Star Wars with inspiring stories of impact intrapreneurs. You'll get to know Corporate Jedi such as Susie Lonie and Nick Hughes, who, while working for Vodafone in Kenya, introduced a mobile payment method which brought financial inclusion to millions; Myriam Sidibé at Unilever, who turns making soap into saving lives; and Gib Bulloch, founder of Accenture Development Partnerships, which provides first-class consulting services to NGOs leveraging their impact. With actionable advice, such as how to create a business case, how to measure social impact, and more, the book is not only an entertaining read but also helps executives apply insights to their own daily work.

Written for leaders, managers, and all professionals looking to create positive impact through their work, this book will give future Corporate Jedi the courage and tools to use the force of business for good.

Heiko Hosomi Spitzeck co-founded the first Executive Education Center on Impact Intrapreneurship at Fundação Dom Cabral in Brazil. Here and in collaboration with the League of Intrapreneurs, Yunus Social Business, and the World Economic Forum he challenges employees to become impact intrapreneurs.

"An indispensable resource for change makers within big business."

Denise Hills, *board member, UN SDG Pioneer*

"Heiko Hosomi Spitzeck's new book, *The Corporate Hero's Journey: Your Path to Being an Impact Intrapreneur*, is a fun read with the deeply serious intention of releasing the power of intrapreneurship on the world's most serious problems. The need is so dire that his light hearted approach is the best way to approach it, hiding essential advice in the story of the Star Wars Jedi.

If you are a frustrated innovator struggling to do good through business, this book is for you. Our current challenges from climate change to food shortages, from AI to managing water shortages, now demand a step change in the rate of innovation. For this we need an army of intrapreneurs. They require focusing much of that innovation on what matters most. If you are up for the challenge, this book will guide you through finding a way to succeed in making the world a lot better in ways that work for your employer."

Gifford Pinchot III, *author, serial intrapreneur, consultant, thought leader; co-originator of the term "Intrapreneur"*

THE CORPORATE HERO'S JOURNEY

Your Path to Being an Impact Intrapreneur

Heiko Hosomi Spitzeck

Routledge
Taylor & Francis Group
LONDON AND NEW YORK

This book has not been endorsed by Lucasfilm, Disney or its associates.

Designed cover image: Getty Images

First published 2024
by Routledge
4 Park Square, Milton Park, Abingdon, Oxon OX14 4RN

and by Routledge
605 Third Avenue, New York, NY 10158

Routledge is an imprint of the Taylor & Francis Group, an informa business

British Library Cataloguing-in-Publication Data
A catalogue record for this book is available from the British Library

Library of Congress Cataloging-in-Publication Data
Names: Spitzeck, Heiko, author.
Title: The corporate hero's journey : your path to being an impact intrapreneur / Heiko Hosomi Spitzeck.
Description: Abingdon, Oxon ; New York, NY : Routledge, 2024. | Includes bibliographical references.
Identifiers: LCCN 2023047691 (print) | LCCN 2023047692 (ebook) | ISBN 9781032615073 (hardback) | ISBN 9781032579030 (paperback) | ISBN 9781032615080 (ebook)
Subjects: LCSH: Social entrepreneurship. | Social responsibility of business. | Management—Social aspects. | Star Wars films—Influence.
Classification: LCC HD60 .S6733 2024 (print) | LCC HD60 (ebook) | DDC 658.4/092—dc23/eng/20240131
LC record available at https://lccn.loc.gov/2023047691
LC ebook record available at https://lccn.loc.gov/2023047692

ISBN: 978-1-032-61507-3 (hbk)
ISBN: 978-1-032-57903-0 (pbk)
ISBN: 978-1-032-61508-0 (ebk)

DOI: 10.4324/9781032615080

Typeset in Garamond
by Apex CoVantage, LLC

Contents

Acknowledgments

To my wife Marise and my son Otto – and the amazing journey of our little family.

To my team at the Center of Intrapreneurship at FDC, Alda Marina Campos, Juliana Travassos, and Pablo Handl for their continuous support, constructive critique, and friendship.

To the League of Intrapreneurs and all the wonderful people I met there, who continue to inspire, teach, and challenge me.

To Muhammad Yunus, the humblest, most human, inspiring, and impactful Peace Nobel Laureate I've ever met.

To Peter Ulrich and my friends at oikos International, who introduced me to the way of the force.

To Guido Palazzo, who continuously keeps me aware of the dark side.

To Fundação Dom Cabral in Brazil, which allows me to be myself and challenges me to become a better teacher, every day.

To Elisa Alt at Kings College London, a Jedi Master in academia who made this book possible.

To Rebecca Marsh and Lauren Whelan, my publishers, and the amazing team at Routledge.

To you! Embarking on a journey that might take you into the outer rim of the galaxy.

Introduction

THESE ARE DARK TIMES . . .

The evidence of climate change is everywhere, from burning forests in California to the low river levels in Germany. The extinction of species and biodiversity is advancing, causing diseases like Covid to spread from animals to humans. The pandemic has taken back poverty reduction advances by ten years in Brazil[1] and extreme weather events led to the displacement of nearly 25 million people in 2019 alone.[2] Expectations are that in 2050, we will have more plastic than fish in our oceans, and already today an average American ingests between 74,000 and 121,000 microplastic particles every year.[3] All this because an **Empire of Corporate Actors** insists on ever rising quarterly profits.

Executives driven by the **dark side** are using business for personal gain, neglecting the impacts on humans and nature. In their view, everything turns into a resource to be exploited – be it human or natural resources. They focus on maintaining the system and managed to establish economic theories supporting this approach, institutionalizing shareholder-value maximization, not only in business education, but in laws. Today, very few politicians are questioning the necessity for continuous growth. It has become an ideology, which the American author Edward Abbey once described as: "growth for the sake of growth is the ideology of the cancer cell."[4] Dark times indeed . . .

. . . BUT THERE IS A NEW HOPE . . .

The lack of purpose beyond profits is causing millions of people to leave the corporate machinery. Companies are feeling the impact of the "Great Resignation" and struggle with new strategies of "Employer Branding" to attract younger generations, which are not buying anymore into "losing life in the office" for their monthly pay checks. They don't want to be seen and treated as simple Human Resources. But also, among the people who are not leaving their employers, a **new breed of Jedi knights is emerging – the Corporate Jedi**. They use **the force** of business for good. Here are some of the Corporate Jedi Masters you'll get to know more about in this book:

- **Susie Lonie** and **Nick Hughes** were working for Vodafone in Kenia. They realized that roughly 20% of the population had access to financial services. Eighty percent of the population was financially excluded; they did not have a current account, debit, or credit card. Their idea? M-Pesa: a mobile payment solution that allows users to send and receive money just like text messages. As more than 60% of the population had mobile phones, the new service spread like wildfire, bringing financial inclusion to millions – while at the same time generating a new revenue stream for Vodafone. Based on this project they were awarded with the Economist's Social and Economic Innovation Award in 2010.
- At first sight, you might think that **Myriam Sidibé** at Unilever simply sells soap. If you, like 1.3 million others, listen to her TED talk, you quickly discover that it's not about selling soap, it's all about saving lives – especially the lives of 6.6 million children who do not reach their fifth birthday, as many die due to a lack of hygiene. Her talk has become a standard for showing new Corporate Jedi how to do the perfect pitch, as she blends the business case and social impact in a very convincing narrative.
- **Gib Bulloch** was working at Accenture and never thought that his business skills could be used to foster local development, until he volunteered in Macedonia helping SMEs in business planning. Once he was back from his sabbatical, he founded Accenture Development Partnerships, which is providing first-class consulting services to NGOs and development organizations such as UNICEF, WWF, Oxfam and others, thus leveraging their positive impacts.

While Luke Skywalker was fighting with his lightsaber, these Corporate Jedi use empathy, human-centred design, the theory of change, the Sustainable Development Goals from the United

Nations, storytelling and, of course, business plans and corporate objectives to create more humane and sustainable businesses.

Just as members of the **Rebellion in Star Wars** were spread in space during the Empire, these Corporate Jedi are spread in thousands of organizations globally. Most of them feel alone, isolated, and tired of swimming against the traditional corporate currents. It can be a lonesome fight, but it needn't be! It's time to bring the Corporate Jedi together, show them that they are not alone, train them, and equip them with the tools they need to transform business to serve humanity and the planet, instead of destroying them. Provide them with a place where they can rest, cure their wounds, and nurture their resilience. Connecting and strengthening them is the only hope to form a Rebel Alliance strong enough to impact business beyond isolated projects, to turn corporations into platforms that foster the common good, and give a human face to capitalism as we know it. If this call is for you, get in touch. The **Corporate Rebel Alliance** is recruiting!

NOTES

1 The World Bank. (2023, October 9). *Brazil – overview. The World Bank.*
2 UNHCR. (2024, January 26). *How climate change impacts refugees and displaced communities.* UNHCR.
3 Weston, P. (2019, June 5). Average person consumes up to 120,000 particles of microplastics every year. *The Independent*. London.
4 Abbey, E. (1977). *The journey home: Some words in the defense of the American West.* Plume.

THE HERO'S JOURNEY

Did you know that the Star Wars saga is based on the hero's journey by Joseph Campbell? Campbell was professor of literature and studied comparative mythology and religion. He discovered that all great myths follow very similar patterns which he described as the hero's journey in his book *The Hero with a Thousand Faces.*[1] While published already in 1949, the book entered the *New York Times* bestseller list in 1988, after a series of interviews with Campbell broadcasted by PBS – known as the Moyers interviews. As George Lucas was an avid admirer of Campbell's work, he used the hero's journey as a template for the Star Wars storyline. Both later became friends and in the commemorative edition of the book, published by Princeton University Press, George Lucas writes:

> In the three decades since I discovered *The Hero with a Thousand Faces*, it has continued to fascinate and inspire me. Joseph Campbell peers through centuries and shows us that we are all connected by a basic

DOI: 10.4324/9781032615080-1

> need to hear stories and understand ourselves. As a book, it is wonderful to read; as illumination into the human condition, it is a revelation.[2]

Campbell traced myths in different regions (from Bali, to India, to Argentina), epochs (from Babylonia, ancient Egypt, and Rome to modern day Norway) and found that storytelling is universal and that it follows a common recipe he called the **monomyth** (a term which he borrowed from James Joyce). Campbell described the ever-repeating structure of stories and myths the following way:

> A hero ventures forth from the world of common day into a region of supernatural wonder: fabulous forces are there encountered, and a decisive victory is won: the hero comes back from this mysterious adventure with the power to bestow boons on his fellow man.[3]

The hero's journey is originally divided in 17 stages and three main acts (departure, initiation, return) and usually displayed as a circle. As the hero or heroine grows during the journey, I prefer to display it in the following way.

The hero's journey is about a protagonist who leaves their known world for the realm of extraordinary happenings, learns something about themselves, and returns with that knowledge to the benefit of their society. Campbell taught that along the journey the hero undergoes a significant personal transformation. The heroine or hero starts in their ordinary world, and their current view of the world gets scattered, before they pass through challenging tests, harvest their boon, and end up on a higher level back in the ordinary world. While the journey often starts with the hero's desire to change the world, they realize that, in order to change the world, you first need to understand yourself – or as the ancient Greek would say: know thyself. For those who embark on this journey, Campbell offers links to Jungian psychology, religion, and spiritualism – something quite advanced and courageous for his time.

His work turned out to be the founding stone of storytelling techniques. The hero's journey has become a standard reference in writing and film, influencing e.g., filmmakers such as Christopher Vogler (*The Lion King*) and writers such Dan Brown (*The DaVinci Code*).

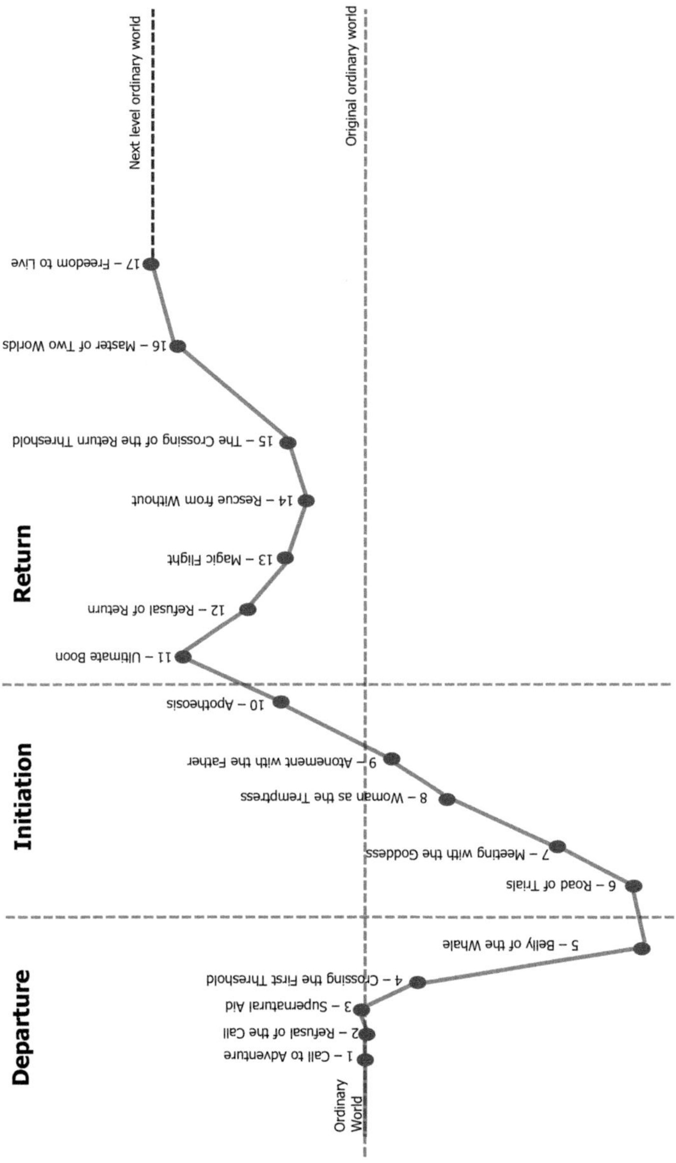

Figure 0.1 The heroine's/hero's journey

Most of the intrapreneurs presented in this book deeply connect to the logic of the hero's journey and would probably agree that their journey was primarily a journey of personal transformation. In episode 1 of the Bill Moyers interviews, Campbell says: "we all operate in society in relation to a system. Now is the system going to eat you up and relieve you of your humanity or are you going to be able to use the system to human purposes."[4] This book features the journeys of Corporate Jedi who have been able to use the economic system to human purposes.

In the following, each stage of the hero's journey is presented with a reference to Campbell's work and exemplified by the Star Wars saga – primarily following the adventures of Luke Skywalker. After that, an example of an impact intrapreneur at the very same stage is provided together with some reflections and tools that help you to identify if you have arrived at this stage in your journey and how to prepare for the next stage of your adventure.

NOTES

1 See Campbell, J. (1949). *The hero with a thousand faces.* Pantheon Books.
2 Campbell, J. (2004). *The hero with a thousand faces: Commemorative edition.* Princeton University Press.
3 Campbell, J. (1949). *The hero with a thousand faces.* Pantheon Books.
4 Taken from episode one of the Bill Moyers interviews available at Lorber, K. (2023, August 23). *Joseph Campbell and the power of the myth – ep. 1: "The hero's adventure"* [Video]. YouTube. https://www.youtube.com/watch?v=pE8ciMkayVM

Stage 1

THE CALL TO ADVENTURE

The hero's journey starts with the call to adventure in which the hero is faced with an event, conflict, problem, or challenge that makes them begin their adventure. Embarking on the journey they leave the ordinary world behind and is thrown outside the comfort zone.

Remember in *Star Wars: Episode IV – A New Hope* Luke Skywalker finds a hidden message within R2D2 and follows the sympathetic and persistent robot to meet Obi-Wan Kenobi. The old Jedi gives Luke Skywalker his father's lightsaber and later tells him: "you must learn the ways of the force, if you want to come with me to Alderaan."[1]

In a very similar way, the journey of impact intrapreneurs starts with a call to adventure. Gib Bulloch founded Accenture Development Partnership (bringing professional consulting services to leverage the impact of third-sector organizations) and his journey started during an underground train ride to work when he

DOI: 10.4324/9781032615080-2

came across an announcement looking for business professionals helping to rebuild the economy in ex-Yugoslavia after the war.

Campbell writes that the call to adventure as understood by myth is the "awakening of the self" in which the hero realizes that he can have an impact on the world. It usually happens in the moment, in which "the familiar life horizon has been outgrown; the old concepts, ideals, and emotional patterns no longer fit; the time for passing of a threshold is at hand."[2]

So how do you recognize that your call to adventure is close?

- Your ordinary world has become dull, and you are looking for a change.
- You are concerned about social and or environmental impacts related to business-as-usual.
- A new approach, inspiring leader, new way of doing things is capturing your attention.

Useful questions to accelerate this process:

- Think about people who truly inspire you.
- If you knew you could not fail – what would you do?
- If you were to write a book about improving the state of the world and with a guarantee to become a best-seller – what would it be about?
- Who were your heroes when you were a child? What attracted you to them?
- If you had one year off with no concern about money – how would you spend your time?

MEET YOUR JEDI MASTER: GIB BULLOCH

Gib Bulloch was born in the late 1960s on the Isle of Bute in Scotland. At the age of 12 he was diagnosed with alopecia, losing all his hair, which – in his words – taught him that he "was used of being the odd one out from an early age."[3] He studied Naval Architecture and Offshore Engineering and later completed an MBA at the University of Strathclyde and a post-grad course on

Cross Sectoral Partnerships at the University of Cambridge. After starting his career at BP and later working at Mars, he joined Accenture in 1996.

It was one of these typical days, in which thousands of people pour into the London Underground in the morning, making their way to work. Nothing indicated that this day would be a game-changer for Gib. As usual he started reading the *Financial Times* on the tube – as Londoners call their Underground Transport, just as many others in the city, when suddenly his eyes fell on a posting by VSO (Voluntary Service Overseas). They were looking for individuals with business skills to assist in local development initiatives. He thought: "isn't development something for doctors, nurses, and teachers? Why are they looking for businesspeople like me?" and pondered: "might this at last be the meaning I'd been missing in my career today?"

After spending a sabbatical year on a VSO engagement in Macedonia, helping SMEs with their business planning and fostering local economic development, Gib was back in Accenture's offices in London. His "epiphany moment" made him a different person as he later reflected: "it was an experience that would not only change my career but also has had a profound impact on my life and, I believe, on the life of many others."[4] He was wondering: "what if Accenture could provide first-class consulting services to NGOs, thus leveraging their impact?"[5]

But how could he convince Accenture's Senior Leaders of his idea? He shaped the idea into a fake press article in which Accenture's Chairman receives public recognition at the World Economic Forum in Davos for leveraging the impact of development organizations and sent it to him. This got him a lunch invitation, and this is also how Accenture Development Partnerships (ADP) was born in 2002 – today an award-winning non-for-loss business within Accenture. ADP has supported the work of organizations such as UNICEF, Oxfam, World Health Organization, WWF, Rockefeller Foundation, and many more. Facilitated by ADP, Accenture's top performing talents embarked on missions to use modern information technology to improve child sponsoring, improve UNICEFs logistics to deliver vaccines, or train thousands of Kenyan nurses using eLearning platforms. ADP grew to successfully deliver a quarter of a billion dollars' worth if aid in over 70 of the poorest countries in the world. Gib had created a Corporate Social Enterprise within Accenture and created his own job as Managing Director Accenture Development Partnerships.

Now I know Gib will say reading this chapter: "I get a lot of recognition, perhaps more than my fair share, given ADP was a team effort."[6] Which leads us to the . . .

Corporate Jedi Insights:

- Be humble – sharing the glory with the team is important, as first (and second, and third etc.) followers are as important as someone starting an initiative. I learnt this in a funny leadership lesson video on "First Follower – Leadership Lessons from (a) Dancing Guy". Have a look!
- The purpose – and thus the power and resilience – of a Corporate Jedi is intrinsically linked to serving others, especially the disadvantaged and weak. Therefore, Corporate Jedi use business only to serve other humans; their approach is human centred as opposed to profit focussed.
- Be bold – writing a fake newspaper article and sending it to the chairman of the board requires courage as you are easily labelled as "the odd one." Good that Gib was used to being seen that way!
- It's always good to get out of your comfort zone, to learn how to better serve people. Gib's volunteering year was life changing.

NOTES

1 Luke Skywalker in Lucas, G. (Director). (1977). *Star wars: Episode IV – a new hope* [Film]. 20th Century-Fox.
2 Campbell, J. (1949). *The hero with a thousand faces*. Pantheon Books.
3 G. Bulloch (personal communication, November 2, 2022).
4 G. Bulloch (personal communication, November 2, 2022).
5 G. Bulloch (personal communication, November 2, 2022).
6 G. Bulloch (personal communication, November 2, 2022).

Stage 2

REFUSAL OF THE CALL

When Luke Skywalker gets the invitation to follow Obi-Wan Kenobi to Alderaan he rejects saying: "I can't. I have work to do. It's not that I like the Empire – I hate it, but there is nothing I can do about it right now."[1]

This is the second step in the hero's journey; Joseph Campbell calls it "the refusal of the call."[2] It is his common world that holds the hero back, his work, his role, his friends, his comfort zone. This refusal affirms that the hero is just like you and me, prone to the same doubts and fears.

The same happens to emerging intrapreneurs who perceive themselves as employees. You often hear them say: "I need to do my job and maintain my salary." In most companies, employees have gone through a long, tough process that involves hard study at top schools in order to be selected for a function within the corporation. They all have duties to attend to. For exercising their job function these employees receive decent salaries, benefits, and development opportunities. As they are young in their

DOI: 10.4324/9781032615080-3

careers, they have bills to pay, debt to get rid of, and savings to make – all social pressures that aim to keep people fulfilling their roles within the corporate empire.

This makes turning intrapreneur a dangerous endeavour. An intrapreneur steps out of their job function and takes on things nobody pays them for or wants to. Many intrapreneurs face questions such as: why are you doing this? What's the point? Why don't you stay on track with your career path? Apart from risking your hard-earned status-quo, the corporate immune system is likely to attack you with the power equivalent to the Empire in Star Wars. Companies are organizations – they like to organize stuff; they like things to function. Intrapreneurs who partially stop functioning in their job duties and take on new adventures face resistance from their organization.

You probably are at this stage if you:

- Really would enjoy working on your purpose-project but heard yourself saying things like: "I can't afford to lose my salary," "I'd really love to work in this area, but my day-job does not leave me any time," "I can do this later in my career, after I . . ."
- Feel that you are not in control of your life, as you are trying to attend different demands from other people (boss, colleague, partner, kids etc.)

You're only able to move on if you are taking back control of your own agenda. Think about the stuff you are doing at work. Then decide – is this something I care about, only my employer cares about, or we both care about? The last is the easiest, as is the perfect space where the interest of yourself and your employer overlaps. The tricky part is the work your employer sends your way, but you're not really interested in. Here you can try to delegate to others or negotiate. Finally, try to set some time apart, so you can dedicate yourself to the things you care about. The following literature might help provide some further insights on how to regain control over your agenda:

- Covey, S. R. (1989). *The 7 habits of highly effective people*. Free Press.

- Manson, M. (2018). *The Subtle Art of Not Giving a F*ck: A Counterintuitive Approach to Living a Good Life.* HarperOne.

CORPORATE JEDI PHILOSOPHY: ACT!

> These are dark times.[3]

Indeed, these are dark times. The Stockholm Resilience Centre estimates that four out of nine planetary boundaries have been exceeded.[4] Our demand for food, water, and natural resources is causing irreversible loss of biodiversity and ecosystem services. Human-made emissions will cause sea levels to rise, affecting millions of people and causing new streams of migration. All these issues are increasing the risk that our planet becomes a much less hospitable one, causing more poverty and loss of quality of life even in developed countries.

And most of the corporate world still continues business as usual. Paul Paulman, ex-CEO of Unilever, voiced his growing concern in an event hosted by Yunus Social Business in January 2023 after he had attended the World Economic Forum:

> We are at a delicate time. Governments are not working together. A lot of companies are talking the talk, but not walking the walk. There is an immense gap between what the world needs, and the commitment made by CEOs. Additionally, there is an equally huge gap between what CEOs promise and what they deliver.[5]

Asked about what is needed to change the current state of affairs, Polman responded: "at the end of the day it's leadership. We have the money, we have the technology, but we need people to act."[6]

Corporate Jedi act! They are the leaders we are waiting for and you can be one of them.

We know the challenge is daunting! Rix road is the final episode of *Andor* Season 1.[7] In a moment of despair, Cassian Andor reads a manifest written by Nemik – one of the more philosophical rebels who got killed during their escape from Ferrix. His manifest starts recognizing the power of the enemy – in fact of any authoritarian regime: "alone, unsure, dwarfed by the scale of the enemy."[8] He injects hope by saying "Freedom is a pure idea. It occurs spontaneously and without instruction."[9] Just like intrapreneurs working isolated in different companies he points out that "random acts of insurrection"[10] are happening every day, everywhere in the galaxy and that there are "whole armies, battalions that have no idea that they're already enlisted in the cause."[11] Most intrapreneurs have no idea how many others are doing similar work in other organizations – there are thousands of them. Nemik predicts that a day will come in which there is one too many act of insurrection and that "one single thing will break the siege."[12] This could be yours!

So, what are you waiting for? Act!

MEET YOUR JEDI MASTER: CATHERINE CONNORS

Catherine Connors likes metamorphoses. In her past she was an academic doing her master's thesis on storytelling – more precisely on how stories were told from ancient times to days of the internet. Upon Emilia (her first daughter) being born, her feminist spirit started to flourish, and she became particularly attentive to which gender messages her daughter received by the books they read, the movies they watched, or the digital media they consumed. Teaching political philosophy and social theory at the University of Toronto, her research focused on how digital media was becoming a new form of storytelling especially for women. To better understand this community, she opted to become part of it, launching her blog "Her Bad Mother" in 2006. Somehow unexpected, her blog on parenting became one of TIME's magazines best blogs of 2012 and turned out to be much more lucrative than the salary she earned as a lecturer. So, she became a social media specialist with a particular feminist view on parenting.

In 2011, she met the founders of Babble Media – a magazine and blog directed toward young, educated, urban parents. Babble was broadening its network on storytellers and Catherine was invited to become their Editor in Chief. When Babble was bought by Disney later the same year, she became Head of Content for Disney Interactive. Due to her studies, she was critical of Disney – especially about the gender messages the company sent about princesses. In contrast to other people dreaming about working at Disney, this was never her objective – as she says: "there was a running joke between me and my colleagues because I was the most unlikely Disney executive ever. Disney bought Babble and so they ended up with me."[13]

In late 2011, topics such as gender issues, feminism, and others did not yet rank high on the corporate agenda. Catherine remembers talking about how moms are concerned about the images their daughters received by Disney, upon which some executives said: "nobody listens to moms."[14] She, however, sensed an opportunity here to take her passion and drive change. If you had to choose a place on earth where you could influence how storytelling shapes the dreams and imagination of girls and boys alike – where would you go? Disney! And she had three superpowers at her disposal: 1 – the Babble team was the golden child and brought in as experts on digital, moms, and families. 2 – she was not concerned about being fired as she had a two-year limited contract (okay, she stayed four years in total – but voluntarily). 3 – her passion. Despite all the metamorphoses from academic, to blogger, to digital media, to corporate life, her passion for feminism and storytelling was just getting stronger.

Today, you can see that Disney changed its approach to storytelling and female protagonists. Ten years ago, it would have been impossible to launch *The Little Mermaid* with a black protagonist. The live-action *Cinderella* launched in 2015 portrays a much stronger and refined character than the ancient versions of the classic fairytale. *Frozen* does not have the traditional romantic ending. Even the Star Wars saga is enriched by female protagonists such as Jyn Erso and Rey. These characters no longer follow the traditional recipe of princess being rescued by the hero.

Now how did Catherine help Disney to get there? Guess what: storytelling! The risk framing of the story goes – among young, educated, urban parents Disney is turning into the villain, maintaining antiquated beauty ideals (as you can see by Barbie sales going down) and picturing women as dependent and needing to be rescued. Society is changing, women are getting ever more into powerful positions, and moms do not want to educate their daughters to be princesses, but CEOs, presidents, astronauts, and whatever they would like to become. Then she asked: how can we make sure that Disney becomes the hero of this story?

At this point she suggested a different story: Disney is the guardian of fairytales and stories that are able to spark imagination and picture a different future . . .

By portraying women in line with new societal values, Disney is doing justice to its role as a global cultural institution – and by the way, it's better business, too.

Corporate Jedi Insights:

- If you are thinking about quitting your job – hold on just a second. One of the superpowers of intrapreneurs is not being concerned about being fired. If the situation is not too bad, before you quit – try to change the organization to the better; use it as a platform for change. The worst thing that can happen is that you are getting fired (something you wanted anyhow). While you are pushing for change, I guarantee that you learn more about organizational behaviour, corporate politics, and business in general than any MBA can teach you (as a business school professor, I should not be saying this).
- Storytelling is a weapon – use it! If you need help consult with people like Catherine.

NOTES

1 Luke Skywalker in Lucas, G. (Director). (1977). *Star wars: Episode IV – a new hope* [Film]. 20th Century-Fox.
2 Campbell, J. (1949). *The hero with a thousand faces.* Pantheon Books.
3 Luke Skywalker in Lucas, G. (Director). (1977). *Star wars: Episode IV – a new hope* [Film]. 20th Century-Fox.
4 Stockholm Resilience Centre. (2023). *Planetary boundaries.* Azote for Stockholm Resilience Centre.
5 Yunus Social Business. (2023). Business as a Force for Good – A Transformation Framework for Leaders. 24 January.
6 Stockholm Resilience Centre. (2023). *Planetary boundaries.* Azote for Stockholm Resilience Centre.
7 Gilroy, T. (Writer), & Caron, B. (Director) (2022, September 23). Season 1, Episode 12 [TV series episode]. In S. Wohlenberg, T. Gilroy, K. Kennedy, D. Luna, T. Haynes, & M. Rejwan (Executive Producers), *Andor.* Lucasfilm.

[8] Gilroy, T. (Writer), & Caron, B. (Director) (2022, September 23). Season 1, Episode 12 [TV series episode]. In S. Wohlenberg, T. Gilroy, K. Kennedy, D. Luna, T. Haynes, & M. Rejwan (Executive Producers), *Andor.* Lucasfilm.
[9] Gilroy, T. (Writer), & Caron, B. (Director) (2022, September 23). Season 1, Episode 12 [TV series episode]. In S. Wohlenberg, T. Gilroy, K. Kennedy, D. Luna, T. Haynes, & M. Rejwan (Executive Producers), *Andor.* Lucasfilm.
[10] Gilroy, T. (Writer), & Caron, B. (Director) (2022, September 23). Season 1, Episode 12 [TV series episode]. In S. Wohlenberg, T. Gilroy, K. Kennedy, D. Luna, T. Haynes, & M. Rejwan (Executive Producers), *Andor.* Lucasfilm.
[11] Gilroy, T. (Writer), & Caron, B. (Director) (2022, September 23). Season 1, Episode 12 [TV series episode]. In S. Wohlenberg, T. Gilroy, K. Kennedy, D. Luna, T. Haynes, & M. Rejwan (Executive Producers), *Andor.* Lucasfilm.
[12] Gilroy, T. (Writer), & Caron, B. (Director) (2022, September 23). Season 1, Episode 12 [TV series episode]. In S. Wohlenberg, T. Gilroy, K. Kennedy, D. Luna, T. Haynes, & M. Rejwan (Executive Producers), *Andor.* Lucasfilm.
[13] C. Connors (personal communication, June 29, 2023).
[14] C. Connors (personal communication, June 29, 2023).

Stage 3

SUPERNATURAL AID

As soon as a hero commits to their journey, a guide and magical helper appears. This mentor or master will frequently gift the hero or heroine with a talisman or artifact that will help them later.

For Luke Skywalker, his first supernatural assistance came from Obi-Wan Kenobi, from whom he received his father's lightsabre – the weapon of a Jedi Knight. Obi-Wan's superpowers become evident as soon as they reach Alderaan and find a Stormtrooper patrol. Using the Force, he makes the patrol chief say: "we don't need to see their identification. These are not the droids we're looking for. They can go about their business." Luke stares at him, saying: "I don't understand how we managed to pass through those troops. I thought we'd be dead"[1] to which Obi-Wan responds: "the Force can have a strong influence upon the weak."[2]

Every intrapreneur I've met so far has had some supernatural assistance. For Lucas Urbano, then at Danone, it was a former boss who told him:

DOI: 10.4324/9781032615080-4

> Lucas, you don't need to continue the presentation. I need to make it clear that I love this project, I really think it can be a major opportunity, look at the other companies making direct sales to microentrepreneurs, I love it. . . . But you are proposing something small, focusing on tiny problems, lack of resources to purchase a computer, a manager that skipped the meeting. I put to you the following challenge: if I give you all the money you need, if I allocate my team to help you, make sure that they are committed . . . which project would you give me? Instead of the 20 women you work with today, how much time and resources would you need to put 500 women in your project? 1000 women? Act in the 10 biggest favelas in Brazil? Because, if the project is good, solid, and ambitious enough, resources won't be scarce. The resource is created when a project delivers what we want.[3]

Of course, help to an intrapreneur isn't in fact supernatural, but it is essential: many times, these first masters or mentors believe in the intrapreneur's potential and challenge them to do better. They share tricks and tips of how to navigate the organization's political system, open doors, mediate conflicts, and have skills the young ones haven't mastered yet.

Lucas remembered: in another moment the same mentor told me: "we see others as greater than they really are, and in contrast, we see ourselves as smaller than we really are."[4] Over the years, I realized that we are usually the first to create our own limits; getting started has more to do with courage and daring than with talent.

How to know you are currently at this stage:

- You accepted a new adventure
- Someone more senior believes in you and helps as well as challenges you to advance and grow as a person and professional. They not only give you technical advice but also provide insights for your life.

Now ask yourself, young apprentice:

Who believes in you and is your mentor? Who challenges you to grow beyond your current level? Who was your first master or mentor; can you reconnect? Or – if you haven't begun your adventure yet – who could it be? What is their "supernatural power"; what can you learn from them or use in favour of your adventure? Why not invite this person for a lunch, coffee, or dinner to simply say "thank you" and tell them what you learnt from them? A little recognition will foster the light side of the force between the two of you and re-energize your mentor. To encourage you to share this energy, have a look at the following video on YouTube entitled "An Experiment in Gratitude – The Science of Happiness" and – if you want – follow their instructions as if you were a participant of the study.[5]

MEET YOUR JEDI MASTER: LUCAS URBANO

In 2007, the CEO of Danone, Frank Riboud, declared that the company would reduce its emissions by 30% until 2012. To make this change happen, 30% of the bonus of the executive team was dependent on achieving this target. Suddenly, Danone operations all around the world were in need to create a robust programme of measuring and reducing emissions. This came to the advantage of Lucas Urbano, who at the time applied to Danone's trainee programme in Brazil, as he was trained in Life Cycle Analysis (LCA).

Using his skills, he worked with different departments within Danone to first measure emissions, define reduction targets, and evaluate results. To guarantee the engagement of different business areas, Lucas created a team of carbon champions. First, the programme focused on the industrial part, but soon Lucas and his team realized that logistics and packaging had a big impact on emissions. Consequently, the focus shifted from industrial operations to procurement, and they managed to convince major suppliers to join Danone's emission reduction journey. In monthly meetings, results were communicated to the senior leadership team.

Still as trainee he implemented the emission reduction programme which helped the Brazilian operations to reduce emissions by 32% until 2012. Taking advantage of the moment, he also created the first sustainability department in Brazil, became sustainability manager in 2010, was promoted to headquarters in France as Nature Manager in 2014, and became PMO for Climate Strategy in 2016 and Global Procurement Director in 2021. In 2022 he became Head of Regenerative Agriculture and Sustainable Sourcing at Unilever.

Corporate Jedi Insights:

- Job-crafting and quick career progress is possible: Lucas has always remained true to his professional purpose. However, he did not hesitate to take advantage of opportunities. Many times, these opportunities arise in business areas that at first glance do not immediately make sense for your attempt to bring sustainability to the core of the company. This approach also helped him to become a more experienced professional being able to navigate different areas of the business.
- People first! On his LinkedIn profile he argues that only by focusing on people can we save the environment:

> I am working with a wide variety of stakeholders on programmes to implement regenerative farming practices and protect, conserve and restore natural ecosystems. A big part of this is engaging and supporting the suppliers, the farmers and smallholders who are vital to the maintenance of these environments.[6]

CORPORATE JEDI PHILOSOPHY: ECO NOT EGO!

In his first years at Danone, Lucas Urbano worked on a project preserving Brazilian biodiversity in the Atlantic Forest. It was a relaunch of Danoninho (a famous brand targeted toward children) and the narrative was that for every Danoninho consumed, the company would protect one square meter of Amazon forest. The campaign was the most successful rebranding in the history of Danoninho, and Lucas and his team worked very hard to make sure it would.

Soon enough, the campaign was receiving an award from a big supermarket chain, but instead of Lucas, his colleagues at the marketing department were selected to represent Danone. He started to complain to his boss that he wasn't given any recognition by the marketing team, even though he worked so hard on the project, etc.

His boss turned around and said:

> Lucas, you always wanted that your colleagues embrace sustainability and put it into their diaries and priorities. And now, as they are doing exactly that, you want to be in their place? We are a company driven by marketing, they are driving our business, you should be happy that sustainability gets them this visibility. Be careful with your ego! We are here to put sustainability in our day-to-day business and that, ideally, we'll not need any sustainability department in the future. Use these opportunities to engage and inspire more people! What is more important to you? Be at another sustainability event, where you are already known as a change maker, or that you gain an important ally in the marketing department?[7]

As Corporate Jedi we need to remind ourselves, that we are not working for our personal gain or recognition. In this case, it's about the corporate ecosystem. The award is an opportunity to share the glory and win important allies in different parts of the business. Having motivated colleagues puts sustainability transversally in the organization and helps to turn the company into a sustainable corporation. However, for Corporate Jedi it does not stop there, as they work for a healthier ecosystem in general – benefitting stakeholders such as farmers, suppliers, and customers together with protecting the natural environment. Fittingly enough, Danone has an internal investment of € 100 million fund for impact intrapreneurs, which is called "Ecosystem Fund."

Therefore, always remember: eco not ego!

WEAPON: DECODING STRATEGY

Your project needs to become the company's project.

As you embark on your intrapreneurial journey be aware. First-time and young intrapreneurs especially want to push new ideas – and this is completely fine. However, the better you link your project to the organization's existing strategy, the more likely you succeed and the less likely you will be suffering from burn-out. If it is your first time as an intrapreneur within your organization, connecting to corporate targets also signals that you understood what the company is all about, that you help others hit their KPIs (and get their bonus), and that you are a team player. This all creates trust and might enable you to embark on more challenging projects in the future.

You can use a combination of the following tactics to decode strategy:

- Study corporate documents and existing KPIs: Lucas Urbano understood that Danone wanted to progress on climate change and that the bonus of his leaders depended on reducing emissions. This helped him a lot in selling his idea.
- Do an interview with your immediate boss: listen before you sell your idea! Before you try to convince your boss of a particular idea, why not have a coffee and ask open questions such as: what keeps you up at night? If you had U$ 1 million to invest into our business area, what would you spend it on? Which are the most urgent social and environmental issues regarding our business in your point of view? If you return to your boss with a solution to what they are concerned about, your chances for support increase manifold.
- Participate in a call with financial analysts: think about where real business conversations are happening and if you have a chance to participate. Calls with investors are usually a good opportunity to see what gets discussed. Maybe your company gets challenged on its climate action – and opens a door for your project idea.
- Review annual and sustainability reports: a review of reports might indicate which social and environmental issues are on the top of the corporate agenda.
- Analyze leadership talk: Carla Crippa from Ambev analyzed her leader's concerns regarding social and environmental issues. She understood that access to potable water was a key concern, and this helped her to get CEO buy-in by slide 2!
- Do a media review: how is your company or the industry perceived by the media? Which social and environmental challenges are discussed? Any competitors going through

a reputation crisis? Looking at the current public discussion might help to spot issues where the company could use some help.

If you manage to convince yourself that your idea is something of the company's interest, then you are more likely to receive support from leaders across the business and to scale your idea in the future.

NOTES

1 Lucas, G. (Director). (1977). *Star wars: Episode IV – a new hope* [Film]. 20th Century-Fox.
2 Lucas, G. (Director). (1977). *Star wars: Episode IV – a new hope* [Film]. 20th Century-Fox.
3 L. Urbano (personal communication, January 29, 2023).
4 L. Urbano (personal communication, January 29, 2023).
5 Participant. (2013, July 11). *An experiment in gratitude – the science of happiness* [Video]. YouTube. https://www.youtube.com/watch?v=oHv6vTKD6lg&t=6s
6 Urbano, L. (n.d.). About. LinkedIn. Retrieved January 2023. https://www.linkedin.com/in/lucas-urbano/.
7 L. Urbano (personal communication, January 29, 2023).

Stage 4

THE CROSSING OF THE FIRST THRESHOLD

Getting outside your comfort zone? Good!

We have seen how the hero's journey starts with a call to adventure and some supernatural help. However, it's essential that the hero (or heroine) steps outside the comfort zone. Campbell calls this stage the Crossing of the First Threshold and writes: "the adventure is always and everywhere a passage beyond the veil of the known into the unknown; the powers that watch at the boundary are dangerous; to deal with them is risky."[1]

Luke Skywalker crossed the first threshold at Mos Eisely. Standing on a cliff with the robots looking upon the spaceport, Obi-Wan warns him: "you will never find a more wretched hive of scum and villainy."[2] Especially when he enters the Cantina and is attacked, Luke feels that he entered a new world of adventure. Once more, Obi-Wan protects Luke – using his Jedi skills.

DOI: 10.4324/9781032615080-5

In the Bill Moyers interviews, Campbell explains that there are threshold guardians protecting the crossing from the ordinary into the special world. We should not think of it as a physical threshold but rather as a transition from the world we know and take for granted into the unconscious world where the hero meets strange creatures that operate on a completely different logic.

For the two impact intrapreneurs at Coca-Cola in Brazil, Claudia Lorenzo and Pedro Massa, the crossing of the first threshold might have been the moment they took the leadership team into the favelas to find out how the company could help to improve the quality of life of its inhabitants. After getting accustomed to the different environment, understanding local challenges, and looking at the competencies of the company, they founded Coca-Cola Coletivo, a program that has supported more than 256.000 unemployed youngsters in accessing the labour market since 2009.

Priscila Matta, a trained anthropologist, potentially crossed the threshold once she joined the corporate world. She has helped cosmetics company Natura to structure its relationships to communities, which are essential in providing knowledge on how to use Brazilian biodiversity for the company's well-known and successful EKOS line of products.

How to know you are currently at this stage:

- You met a lot of very different people lately: e.g. you started to meet people working in research institutions, regional government, or NGOs.
- You entered new territories, exploring new cultures, languages, and traditional knowledge.
- You are feeling awkward and unsure on how to behave as you operate in new surroundings, which are unfamiliar to you.

First of all: relax and take your time. At this stage it is very counterproductive to rush. Immerse yourself in the new world, understand what motivates the different people you meet, and trust your feelings.

MEET YOUR JEDI MASTERS: CLAUDIA LORENZO AND PEDRO MASSA

Research done in 2008 showed that income improvements in poor communities in Brazil could lead to an increase of beverage consumption of up to 30%. Coca-Cola Brazil, however, did not have effective marketing channels which could reach those communities. Claudia Lorenzo and Pedro Massa worked in marketing and thought about a way to reach those communities while at the same time improving their quality of life. This meant, in a first step, to understand what quality of life really means to people living in low-income communities.

If you don't go, you don't know!

They first prepared 15 executives of the leadership team through discussions with an anthropologist researching low-income communities in Rio de Janeiro, before embarking on a three-day learning journey living into the favelas. The executives lived with local families and established relations with the local community leaders. Their mission: to discover what the community needs to thrive and where Coca-Cola could help by using its corporate competencies. Among the many things they found was a high unemployment rate – especially affecting adolescents – and poor administration of local retailers, both caused by low educational standards.

These insights lead to the creation of Coca-Cola Coletivo – a shared-value platform that trains mainly teenagers in self-management and retail. The Coca-Cola Institute trained local community trainers, who were delivering classes on finance, logistics, and marketing. They learnt, however, that social and self-management skills were even more important to prepare participants for the labour market. Within the programme, participants were challenged to apply the knowledge working at local retailers within the community.

In 2009, Coletivo was operational in four cities and five learning facilities, benefitting roughly 500 participants. In 2013 Coca-Cola counted 500 learning facilities in over 150 cities, training more than 65,000 participants. Until 2021 Coletivo trained more than 300,000 participants and helped more than 80,000 people into formal employment. In the case study "Thirsty for

More – Coca-Cola's Shared Value Approach with Communities across Brazil" published by the Shared Value Initiative they captured some voices of participants of the programme.[3]

Márcia Lima, one of the participants in the aforementioned case study, said: "Coletivo changed so much for me. It showed me what I have inside and that my future depends on me."

All this would not have been possible without attending as well to business objectives. While the average market growth was 6% per year, the consumption of Coca-Cola in communities where Coletivo was present grew 9.5%. Key to this success was the knowledge transfer to local retailers, who started to sell more generally, including Coca-Cola. Of course, brand engagement was also stronger in those communities. These positive business results also supported the growth of the initiative, as the commercial managers at Coca-Cola had a financial interest of bringing Coletivo into their communities. A virtuous circle had been created.

Corporate Jedi Insights:

- If you don't go, you don't know! If you want to help someone, figure out what they really need. The immersion of the executives in the favelas of Brazil was key to the success of the Coletivo initiative.
- Start small and make sure your model is solid before you scale. The measurement of financial as well as social impact indicators is essential in this regard. Do not scale initiatives that are not at least covering their cost.
- Make sure the community has ownership of the project.

WEAPONS: THE BUSINESS CASE

Many people are afraid of numbers and finance. I am too. Honestly, one of my repeating nightmares deals with having to pass a maths exam or everybody will find out that I am a fraud as a professor.

During the daytime, however, I found out that the general logic is not that difficult to understand. Think about it – if you had to invest US $1,000,00 and someone offered to pay you back US $1,100,000 in a year's time and someone else offered you US $1,500,000, where would you invest?

The money you are getting back in a year's time is your return on investment. The formula is:

$$\text{Return on Investment} = \frac{\text{Outcome} - \text{Investment}}{\text{Investment}}$$

In option 1 your return of investment is 10% and in option 2 it's 50%. Where would any rational person invest? Clearly option 2 as it has a higher return.

How do you calculate the return on investment for your intrapreneurial project?

The first question you have to respond to is: how much am I asking for? Here you need to list all the costs you'll have in order to set up your project and to deliver results. These might be hours of work, external support, and some investments for new equipment.

Let's take the example of some very young impact intrapreneurs working in Brazil. They realized that some of the heating for a production process is done by gas. At the same time there are wooden pallets which needed to be discarded at the facility. Their idea: why not substitute the gas boiler by a wood furnace? So here's what their initial investment calculation looked like:

Working hours (80 hours of the team at a cost of US $15.00 an hour)	US	$1,200
Installation firm support and project planning	US	$8,800
A new wood furnace	US	$65,000
Total investment	US	$75,000

So, they were asking for an investment of US $75,000 from their employer. If someone asked you for that much money – what would you say?

This leads us to the second question: how does your organization get its money back? It might be by reducing cost or by generating new revenue.

Back to our example – the team came up with the following numbers:

Annual cost of gas which could be saved	US $135,000
Annual cost of discharging the wooden pallets	US $15,000
Total cost reductions	US $150,000

So, the return on investment was

$$\frac{\text{US } \$150{,}000 - \text{US } \$75{,}000}{\text{US } \$75{,}000} = 100\%$$

If you come up with a return on investment of over 20%, usually your CFO will kiss your feet and ask you: "what took you so long to bring this project to my attention?"

Observations regarding the business case

- The business case is essential, and I am frequently surprised to see pitches where the team does not respond the first question: how much am I asking for? If you are not clear in your pitch on what you want the people to do (how much to invest, which doors to open, where to sign etc.) all your work is in vain.
- Once you ask for some support in your pitch, you also need to answer question 2: what does the person get in return? How are you delivering value to her? Often it's a good exercise to ask yourself: would I invest my money in this project? Would I ask my mother to put her retirement savings into this?
- Before creating hypotheses on what the person wants in return, why not have a coffee and ask her: what are you concerned about? What are the KPIs you need to meet? If you had

US $100 million to invest in the business, where would you put the money and why?
- Adapt your pitch to the person you are talking to. This first means, be sure who are you talking to and what support you want from this person. While the CFO might be interested in the return on investment, the operations manager might be more concerned about not blowing his very limited investment budget, and the sourcing manager more about the development of gas prices in the future.
- Of course, this example of the business case is a very simple one. You can enhance this basic logic with financial criteria such as payback periods and net present value next to different payback scenarios (worst case, normal case, best case). However, if you get this basic logic straight, you just need to drop into your finance department and ask if someone can help you to build your case.

CORPORATE JEDI PHILOSOPHY: TRUST YOUR FEELINGS

In his attack on the Death Star Luke flies into the trench and gets his targeting device up when he suddenly hears Obi Wan's voice in his head: "use the force Luke." Behind him, Darth Vader exclaims: "the force is strong with this one." Luke is hesitant to give up the technological support and trust in the force. In Luke's head Obi Wan continues: "let go. Luke trust me." He switches off his targeting computer, which is noticed by the command post and the officer asks: "you switched off your targeting computer, what's wrong?" He answers: "nothing. I'm all right." Using the force he manages to destroy the death star and again hears the voice of Obi Wan saying: "remember: The force will be with you. Always!"[4]

Who would have made the decision if Luke had used the targeting computer? Luke or the computer? Just like Luke Skywalker, Corporate Jedi will encounter situations in which they are forced to make difficult decisions. It's the freedom of choice – and the consequent responsibilities. If guided by the light side of the force, their "gut feeling" will help them to make an empathic, responsible decision. This capacity will become even more valuable in the future as artificial intelligence such as ChatGPT will definitely be used as a tool for making decisions. If we leave these decisions completely to the computer, we will be giving our responsibility and, finally, our humanity, away.

Simon Sinek's TED talk on "How great leaders inspire action" has been viewed more than 60 million times. One of his insights is that great leaders inspire us, by talking to our emotions and not by providing us convincing evidence and numbers. He explains:

> This is where gut decisions come from. Sometimes you can give somebody all the facts and figures, and they say, "I know what all the facts and details say, but it just doesn't feel right." Why would we use that verb, it doesn't "feel" right? Because the part of the brain that controls decision-making doesn't control language. The best we can muster up is, "I don't know. It just doesn't feel right." Or sometimes you say you're leading with your heart or soul. I hate to break it to you, those aren't other body parts controlling your behaviour. It's all happening here in your limbic brain, the part of the brain that controls decision-making and not language.[5]

You find the reference to the importance of emotions various times in the Star Wars universe; remember for example the recurring phrase: "I have a bad feeling about this."[6]

So, trusting your feelings is important for decision-making. Corporate Jedi always try to create value for a group of stakeholders, not only for shareholders. This requires empathy. More often than not, "it does not feel right" stems from the perception that one of the stakeholders (normally the weakest) will be hurt – or at least – not benefit from a certain decision. Trusting their feeling therefore is important for bringing this empathy into the decision and considering all of the stakeholders involved.

Another important part of trusting your feelings is simply acknowledging them. Corporate Jedi experience feelings such as frustration, disappointment, and anxiety while pursuing their goals. Trusting your feelings and acknowledging them, rather than suppressing or ignoring them, is the first step to search for support and better manage emotions, e.g., to take a time-out, decelerate, and recharge your energy.

Overall, "trust your feelings" will be a useful reminder for Corporate Jedi to stay connected to their intuition and empathy and to cater to their personal resilience.

NOTES

1 Campbell, J. (1949). *The hero with a thousand faces*. Pantheon Books.
2 Lucas, G. (Director). (1977). *Star wars: Episode IV – a new hope* [Film]. 20th Century-Fox.
3 The complete case study can be found here: Smith, D., Chandrasekhar, R., Parkhurst, M., & Sud, P. (2013). *Thirsty for more – Coca-Cola´s shared value approach with communities across Brazil, shared value initiative*. Further information has been taken from the Portuguese version of Grayson, D., McLaren, M., & Spitzeck, H. (2016). *Intraempreendedorismo social, jazz e outras coisas*. Alta Books.
4 All dialogues taken from Lucas, G. (Director). (1977). *Star wars: Episode IV – a new hope* [Film]. 20th Century-Fox.
5 Sinek, S. (2009, September). *How great leaders inspire action* [Video]. TED Conferences. https://www.ted.com/talks/simon_sinek_how_great_leaders_inspire_action
6 Lucas, G. (Director). (1977). *Star wars: Episode IV – a new hope* [Film]. 20th Century-Fox.

Stage 5

BELLY OF THE WHALE

In Campbell's hero's journey the "Belly of the Whale" is the final stage of departure from the known world. The hero undergoes a metamorphosis which is often seen as being dead and then reborn. The stage "Belly of the Whale" is inspired by the story of Jonah. Called upon by God to travel to Nineveh and warn its inhabitants of divine wrath, Jonah disobeys and takes a ship to Tarshish. As they are caught by a storm due to god's fury, Jonah orders the crew to cast him overboard. He is swallowed by a big fish and in its belly prays for forgiveness. After three days and three nights the fish releases him on the shore. Being "reborn" he goes to Nineveh and disseminates the prophecy as he was told.

Although there is a dispute as to which exact moment represents Luke Skywalker's "Belly of the Whale," I would argue for the scene in which the Death Star's tractor beam takes hold of the Millennium Falcon and literally "swallows" it. How could they possibly win this fight? A crew of three and two droids against

DOI: 10.4324/9781032615080-6

a Death Star full of enemies. Against all odds Luke Skywalker manages to free Princess Leia and is "reborn" as a Jedi apprentice.

Impact intrapreneurs pass through a similar experience. They embark on the adventure of using business as a force for good. In this process the "employee" dies while the "intrapreneur" is born. The combination of the business skills and the recently acquired skills of creating social impact, reconfigure the intrapreneur's professional identity – a process often described as "job crafting" which uses three key traits: values, strengths, and passion.

One powerful example of job crafting is Myriam Sidibé who has worked as "Global Social Mission Director" at Unilever from 2006–2015. In her very inspiring TED talk you will find that in her "Belly of the Whale" experience she entered as a public health professional and came out as a commercial executive trying to sell as much soap as possible. You will also see that she clearly uses three key traits: values, strengths, and passion.

How to know you are currently at this stage:

- You have passed rock bottom.
- The feeling of awkwardness is slowly replaced by playfulness, experimentation, a new strength, and self-awareness.
- You are starting to build and rely on unlikely alliances.

You are at an essential moment of your journey – you're leaving the known world behind. A book which might guide you here is:

- Scharmer, C. O. (2009). *Theory U: Learning from the future as it emerges*. Berrett-Koehler Publishers.

MEET YOUR JEDI MASTER: MYRIAM SIDIBÉ

Myriam Sidibé was born in Mali, one of the poorest countries in the world with an average life expectancy of 58 years in 2020. The surroundings of her upbringing influenced her life trajectory until today and in her TED talk she remembers that "I grew up in a family, in which every dinner conversation was about social justice."[1]

She was trained as an Agricultural and Environmental Engineer from McGill University (Canada), holds a Masters in Water and Waste Engineering from Loughborough University and a Doctorate from the London School of Hygiene and Tropical Medicine. Instead of advancing on her promising academic career, she opted to join Unilever to sell soap. You might ask: how do you become a Corporate Jedi Master by selling soap?

"Bringing affordable and accessible hygiene and nutrition to families across the world has always been my passion,"[2] said Myriam Sidibé.

Unilever provided the perfect platform for her to bring her passion to life. Myriam has become a world leading expert in using brands as a means for positive impact. Unilever's famous Lifebuoy brand was sold in Victorian England in order to fight Cholera. Today, 6.6 million children don't make it to their fifth birthday, and most of these deaths are preventable. If everybody would simply wash their hands, especially birth attendants and families in developing countries, approximately 600,000 deaths could be avoided each year. This is why she spent 15 years of her career at Unilever, in her final time as Global Social Mission Director for the Lifebuoy brand, understanding how to get people to wash their hands. During her journey she not only convinced her leaders at Unilever but also forged private-public partnerships with USAID, the World Bank, WSUP, and many others. She was one of the driving forces behind the creation of Global Handwashing Day, celebrated 15 October, an initiative recognized by the United Nations. While at Unilever, her team's objective was to change the handwashing habits of one billion people. They achieved their goal in 2019.

Since 2018, Myriam concentrated on the power of brands for impact, first as a Senior Fellow at the Harvard Kennedy School's Mossavar Rahmani Center for Business and Government and then by founding "Brands on a Mission." Her book entitled "Brands on a Mission: How to Achieve Social Impact and Business Growth Through Purpose" was published in 2020 by Routledge and won the 2021 AXIOM Business Book Bronze Award. Her 2014 TED

Talk "The Simple Power of Handwashing" has been viewed more than a million times. In the trainings given by the Center of Intrapreneurship her talk is used as the example of the perfect pitch.

Corporate Jedi Insights:

- You can use your employer as a platform for change and to bring *your purpose* to life.
- Make sure your project is attractive to all stakeholders involved. In Myriam's case this meant everybody from the CFO at Unilever to the health ministers of developing countries, a series of multinational NGOs, and international development agencies.
- In many cases, the core purpose can be re-discovered from the founders or when the product was first launched. Lifebuoy was invented to fight cholera; what a perfect starting point for a brand on a mission!
- Think about creating private–public partnerships in order to leverage impact.

WEAPON: STORYTELLING

This book is all about storytelling. By analyzing thousands of stories people have told each other since the beginning of time, Joseph Campbell has provided us with an extensive storytelling template. This template has been taken up by George Lucas in the creation of Star Wars. So, of course, storytelling is in itself a powerful weapon for Corporate Jedi. Why?

Storytelling engages your audience on multiple levels. When we hear stories, we don't just listen to the words – our mind creates mental images; we identify with the characters, feel their emotions, and share their experiences. These features help Corporate Jedi to:

- Inspire and engage: stories help to inspire and engage colleagues, beneficiaries, and other stakeholders in your cause. The stories you tell help to create empathy for the people, whose problem you want to solve.

- Creating a shared vision: stories allow you to design the future you are about to create. They can outline the journey, the potential obstacles, and why it makes sense to overcome them.
- Build credibility: showcasing the impact of the work of Corporate Jedi can help to build credibility and inspire others to embark on their own journey.
- Communicate complex issues: stories allow you to boil down complexity into manageable pieces to allow your audience a better understanding of root causes, challenges, potential solutions, and risks involved.
- Community: sharing stories about failures and success helps to nourish a sense of community among Corporate Jedi.

Our American friends in Hollywood judged Campbell's 17 stages as a little complex. So, they boiled it down to a simpler form – one which became increasingly popular is the storytelling recipe from Pixar. It goes:

1. Once upon a time . . .
2. Every day . . .
3. One day . . .
4. Because of that . . .
5. Because of that . . .
6. Until finally . . .

Now let's take an example of one of the intrapreneurial projects you have seen before. Let's take the example of Myriam Sidibé from Unilever. Her story to get people engaged might have gone like this:

Once upon a time there was a birth attendant in Somalia. Her name was Casho – literally meaning life. Casho was very proud of her skills as she had worked with the most experienced doulas in her community. She saw herself as a carrier assisting new life to be brought to earth and to continue the circle of life of her community and the people openly welcomed her to their houses.

Every day Casho supported pregnant women and their families in preparing for the baby's arrival.
One day, however, everything changed. The baby of a family she attended a few days prior died. Then, so did another little girl she'd helped a week earlier.
Because of that, rumours spread in the community that she was cursed, and that babies she touched were doomed to die.
Because of that, Casho lost not only her standing within the community, but also her livelihood and purpose. Nobody wanted her to be near their families. Every passing day, she felt more isolated and useless to the people she most cared about.
Until finally, people were educated about the necessity of washing hands in the community school. A friend of Casho, who shared her suffering, advised her to assist the handwashing course. As more people got educated about the necessity of washing hands, Casho was able to regain her former position, and became an ambassador for the need to wash hands. She passed on her knowledge to other doulas, and thus saved the lives of many newborns.

Now, if you – working at Unilever – would be able to help Casho, would you? And if she was becoming an ambassador for handwashing because of a Unilever-sponsored event, which soap do you think she would recommend? Now imagine millions of Cashos all over Africa – what would be the impact on public health; what would be the impact on Unilever's sales?

In the episode 1 of the Bill Moyers interviews, Joseph Campbell states: "the main character is a hero or heroine, someone who has found or achieved or done something beyond the normal range of achievement and experience. Someone who has given his life to something bigger than himself or other than himself."[3] This is the mission of Corporate Jedi – give their life and the access to the power of his organization to something bigger than himself and bigger than the quarterly profits. Corporate Jedi help organizations (re-)discover and live up to their purpose! The stories they create are not only suitable tools to "sell" their ideas, but they also provide a convincing narrative and an answer to the question: why does your organization exist?

NOTES

[1] Sidibé, M. (2014, October 14). *Myriam Sidibé: The simple power of handwashing* [Video]. TED Conferences. www.ted.com/talks/ myriam_sidibe_the_simple_power_of_hand_washing?language=en

[2] Sidibé, M. (2014, October 14). *Myriam Sidibé: The simple power of handwashing* [Video]. TED Conferences. www.ted.com/talks/ myriam_sidibe_the_simple_power_of_hand_washing?language=en

[3] Lorber, K. (2023, August 23). *Joseph Campbell and the power of the myth – Ep. 1: "The Hero´s Adventure"* [Video]. YouTube. https://www.youtube.com/watch?v=pE8ciMkayVM

Stage 6

THE ROAD OF TRIALS

Continuing Campbell's hero's journey, the Road of Trials is the first stage of the hero's initiation. In this phase the hero undergoes a series of trials he must survive, in most cases aided by the supernatural aid he encountered before. Inherently the trials are tests of losing yourself for something bigger, a transformation of the consciousness from me to we. Passing through the trials, the hero discovers for the first time his superpowers.

Luke Skywalker's initiation begins on board of the Millennium Falcon. Obi-Wan Kenobi challenges Luke to defend himself against the shots of a small training remote robot using his lightsaber. Putting a helmet on his head and taking Luke's sight, he asks him to reach out into the force and trust his feelings. This, however, is only the first of many trials Luke must survive.

The Young SDG Innovator online program in Brazil can be seen as first steps on the road of trials. Set up by United Nations Global Compact, Fundação Dom Cabral (FDC) and the League of Intrapreneurs, it challenges young talents in corporations to

DOI: 10.4324/9781032615080-7

develop an existing idea on a project that generates value for the company and for society alike. To scale this initiative and to help in the discovery of new projects and stimulate ideas, the Center of Intrapreneurship at FDC created an online course. The final deliverable of the course is a five-minute video pitch in which the participant needs to explain the project, how it adds value to business, and how it delivers progress on the SDGs (Sustainable Development Goals). Pitches are then evaluated by their sponsors as well as experienced intrapreneurs, before the best teams continue their learning journey in an accelerator programme.

Did you ever present a new idea to management? If not, programmes such as the Young SDG Innovators might be a good starting point. Here you'll learn about how to construct a business case, how to measure social and environmental impact, how to navigate corporate politics, and how to construct a convincing narrative for your project. The road of trials is long and plastered with hearing "No's" and overcoming bureaucracy. Well, nobody said that becoming a Corporate Jedi is an easy endeavour. So, if you are developing your idea, testing different pitches and arguments, you are still on the road of trials. Keep up the good work!

And practice is important, as is resistance:

> I went so many times up to the leadership of my organization, until their stock of "No's" ran out.
>
> Humberto Sardenberg, Intrapreneur at Icatu Seguros, Brazil[1]

MEET YOUR JEDI MASTERS: SUSIE LONIE AND NICK HUGHES

> Social Intrapreneurs are unsung heroes.
>
> Susie Lonie[2]

Susie Lonie and Nick Hughes were working for Vodafone and realized that in Kenya, only 2.5 million people out of a population of 39 million had bank accounts. They also knew that Safaricom – the leading telco-provider – had roughly 19 million subscribers. So, they started to ask the typical question of impact intrapreneurs: what if? What if we could offer mobile banking services to the unbanked part of Kenya's population?

This is how M-PESA was born. M stands for mobile and *pesa* means money in Swahili. The platform allows people to send and receive money as easily as sending and receiving text messages. The new service attracted 20,000 subscribers in the month it was launched. The solution is made possible by a partnership between Vodafone and Safaricom. M-Pesa has become the largest mobile money service provider in Africa reaching over 52 million customers in countries such as the Democratic Republic of Congo, Egypt, Ghana, Lesotho, Mozambique, and Tanzania, besides Kenya by 2022. These customers are making over US $314 billion in transactions every year, an impressive case where profits and financial inclusion are clearly aligned. A 2016 article published in *Science* confirmed that M-PESA helped to lift 194,000 households – roughly 2% of the Kenyan population – out of poverty.[3]

The case also showcases the power of digitalization. The United Nations use M-PESA as an example, stating: "the digitalization of finance offers new possibilities for greater financial inclusion and alignment with the 2030 Agenda for Sustainable Development and implementation of the Sustainable Development Goals."[4]

In order to get seed finance for the project, Nick Hughes applied for the UK's Department of International Development's Challenge Fund who was looking for projects using mobile phone technology to support microfinance. His proposal nearly got rejected because some evaluation panel members questioned if it is indeed a good idea to give 1 million GBP of taxpayers' funds to international development of a multinational corporation. We suppose that there were public sector intrapreneurs at play in this critical moment who argued in favour of the project. In an interview after Susie and Nick received The Economist's Social and Economic Innovation Award in 2010, they confessed: "money . . . was the real determining factor for us . . . M-PESA would have never existed had it not been for DFID's Challenge Fund."[5]

Nick also warns of relying on the sustainability department and favours a more business-driven approach: "it's difficult to get buy-in to develop products and services from the Corporate

Responsibility or Corporate Affairs divisions. I knew we had to be in the engine room of the company."[6]

Corporate Jedi Insights:

- You might attract seed finance from outside your company, as in the case of the GBP 1 million financing from DFID. Watch out for impact investors and development agencies – today they are much more open to collaborate with impact intrapreneurs, especially regarding topics such as climate change, clean energy, or circular economy.
- Ideally drive your project out of business. Impact intrapreneurs developing new products, services, and business models must show they bring value to the customers. Corporate functions such as sustainability and institutional relations do not know how to do this and have other KPIs to attend to. Also, if your project makes sense to business, it is much easier to scale.

CORPORATE JEDI PHILOSOPHY: TECH WILL NOT SAVE US

Hope in technology

Some call it "technological utopianism" – an ideology that believes that technology will help us to solve all of our social and environmental problems and lead us to a higher quality of life. This view puts a sugar coating over all problems humankind is facing today and disincentives behavioural changes. Why do I need to change the status-quo? Technology will save us anyway. Remember Darth Vader in *A New Hope* saying: "don't be too proud of this technological terror you've constructed. The ability to destroy a planet is insignificant next to the power of the Force."[7] Reflecting on the potential of technology to save us, Eszter Brhlik holds that the promise of technology has delayed climate action for over 40 years and concludes: "a better world is not coming. We have to create it. And we better do it fast."[8]

Tech is a tool – we need to use it wisely

We need to face the inconvenient truth that we – humans – created the problems, and only we can solve them. Of course, we should use technology to our favour. Now ask yourself, who is in charge of the most significant technological advances? One might argue: the military and business. The first version of the internet was ARPANET an arm of the US Defense Department. The leading robot company Boston Dynamics was initially supported by the Naval Air Warfare Center Training Systems Division; today the main owner is the Hyundai Motor Group. With which objectives are these technological advances being made? Saving the planet is probably one of the less likely answers to this question. Tech is a tool. It's the mindset that is stupid.

Tech needs to stay a tool – subordinated to human decision-making.

On the 30 May 2023, the *New York Times* published an article entitled: "A.I. Poses 'Risk of Extinction,' Industry Leaders Warn." Executives from OpenAI, Google DeepMind, and others warn of the power of artificial intelligence to turn against humanity. Foreseeing the future discussion, Joseph Campbell has already observed: "the question is, does the machine crush humanity, or serve humanity?"[9]

Paul Polman, ex-CEO of Unilever, argues that the key to progress is leadership: "at the end of the day it's leadership. We have the money, we have the technology, but we need people to act."[10] In order for people to act they need the courage to do things differently, they need to have faith in themselves and in their fellow humans. In what do you have faith?

WEAPON: VALUE PROPOSITION CANVAS

> The best thing which can happen to your project is a client threatening to buy your solution.
>
> M. Hunkeler (personal communication, June 26, 2023)

A common challenge during the "Road of Trials" for intrapreneurs is convincing the organization to support the idea. Some apply for internal venture funds, some get seed financing from the sustainability department, but nothing is better than gathering the interest of clients. If a client "threatens" to buy your product or service, how can your leaders say "no"?

And there is a powerful tool called the Value Proposition Canvas. It's part of a more general view on how to build business models, developed by Alexander Osterwalder and Yves Pigneur (see Figure 6.1).[11]

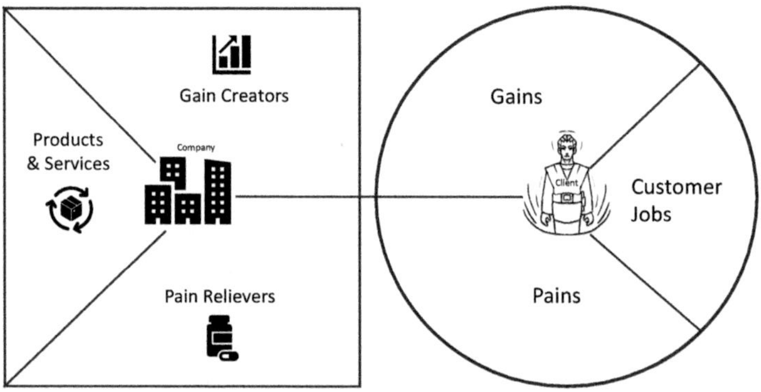

Figure 6.1 Value Proposition Canvas

Source: You can download your version of the Value Proposition Canvas at Osterwalder's company "Strategyzer". Retrieved June 23, 2023, from www.strategyzer.com/canvas/value-proposition-canvas.

The tool challenges you to understand your client and the offered solution (by you or your competitors). First, observe your client (right side of the model) and try to understand:

Jobs to be done – As Harvard professor Clayton Christensen once said: "customers don't buy products. They hire them to do a job."[12] Ask yourself: which "jobs" does your client need to get done? What do they want to achieve in functional, social, and emotional terms? What is the ultimate goal of your client? When and in which context does a client need to do this job?

Pains – what are the clients' pain points? Which negative emotions and stress are caused while trying to get the job done? What obstacles does the client need to overcome? Which problems occur for the client using existing solutions?

Gains – what would delight the client? Which things could be added that increase the pleasure and cause positive emotions while getting the job done?

The left side of the model looks at business solutions – which products and services help the client get their job done? Which are pain relievers and gain creators? Let us take the classical example of comparing Uber to traditional taxi services:

Job to be done – the client wants to get from A to B as smoothly, cheaply, and quickly as possible.

Pains – first, locating a taxi can be difficult which increases the time of getting to the client's destination. Second, as taxi drivers are not evaluated, they might not be as friendly. Third, as the client is travelling in unfamiliar territory the taxi driver might do a detour to charge more.

Pain relievers – by connecting more drivers Uber might be able to provide a ride quicker. By training and ranking drivers, it increases the chances of providing a friendly service. By showing the route and fixing the price at the beginning of travel, Uber increases the trust that drivers will not take a detour.

Gain creators – additionally, drivers might provide sweets or water to make the journey more convenient for clients. Drivers are also trained to ask clients about their preferences regarding conversation, music, and temperature.

The better you understand your client, the more effective your solution will be and the more likely you will convince them to "threaten" your organization to buy your solution! Effective Corporate Jedi might use this canvas for clients as well as for beneficiaries (those you want to help but who don't always have the financial means to "buy" your solution).

NOTES

[1] H. Sardenberg (personal communication, October 28, 2018).

[2] This quote is taken from SustainAbility. (2008). *The social intrapreneur – a field guide for changemakers*. SustainAbility.

[3] The following sources have been used in putting together the first two paragraphs: Vodafone Group. (2021, September 7). *M-Pesa celebrates reaching 50 million customers*. www.vodafone.com/news/services/m-pesa-celebrates-reaching-50-million-customers; and Warner, B. (2022, March 8). More than half of Kenya´s entire GDP is now transacted on this African fintech app. *Fortune*. https://fortune.com/2022/03/08/mpesa-fintech-safaricom-innovation-kenya-africa-mobile-money-unbanked/, as well as Grayson, D, McLaren, M., & Spitzeck, H. (2014). *Social intrapreneurism and all that jazz*. Greenleaf.

[4] See United Nations. (2018). *Financing for development: Progress and prospects 2018*. Report of the Inter-Agency Task Force on Financing for Development.

[5] Grayson, D, McLaren, M., & Spitzeck, H. (2014). *Social intrapreneurism and all that jazz* (p. 73). Greenleaf.

[6] SustainAbility. (2008). *The social intrapreneur – a field guide for corporate changemakers* (p. 56). https://www.allianz.com/content/dam/onemarketing/azcom/Allianz_com/migration/media/current/en/press/news/studies/downloads/thesocialintrapreneur_2008.pdf

[7] Lucas, G. (Director). (1977). *Star wars: Episode IV – a new hope* [Film]. 20th Century-Fox.

[8] Taken from Brhlik, E. (2022). Why technological progress won't save us from a climate disaster. *Medium*. https://medium.com/climate-conscious/why-technological-progress-wont-save-us-from-a-climate-disaster-353ff10e3e08

[9] Taken from episode two of the Bill Moyers interviews available at Lorber, K. (2023, August 23). *Joseph Campbell and the power of the myth – Ep. 2: "the message of the myth"* [Video]. YouTube. https://www.youtube.com/watch?v=Aee5DJ9DSwU

[10] Yunus Social Business. (2023). Business as a Force for Good – A Transformation Framework for Leaders. 24 January.

[11] See Osterwalder, A., & Pigneur, Y. (2010). *Business model generation – a handbook for visionaries, game changers, and challengers*. Wiley.

[12] See Gerdemann, D. (2016, October 4). Clayton Christensen: Customers don't simply buy products – they hire them. *Forbes*. https://www.forbes.com/sites/hbsworkingknowledge/2016/10/04/clayton-christensen-customers-dont-simply-buy-products-they-hire-them/?sh=57cb359cb5cf

Stage 7

THE MEETING WITH THE GODDESS

The meeting with the goddess is the final part of the road of trials. Campbell writes: "the ultimate adventure, when all the barriers and ogres have been overcome, is commonly represented as a mystical marriage of the triumphant hero-soul with the Queen Goddess of the World."[1] The meeting with the goddess is the final test of his talent and required to win the boon.

Luke Skywalker had already seen the goddess as a little image shown by R2D2 to Obi-Wan Kenobi: Princess Leia. While they were trying to escape the Death Star, Luke, Han Solo and Chewbacca discover that Leia is held prisoner and succeed in freeing her, escaping with the Millennium Falcon. By doing so, Luke increased the chances that the construction plans of the Death Star might reach the rebel army and allow them to plan an attack.

For early-stage impact intrapreneurs the first encounter with the goddess might well be represented by the first official yes. After a long road of facing "no's" – imagine colleagues and bosses saying: no, this idea will not work, no we have never done this

DOI: 10.4324/9781032615080-8

before – why now? No, our policies will not allow that . . . the intrapreneur-heroine finally gets a yes: yes, we'll provide seed finance for your project or yes you'll have time to work on this project exclusively. The first little yes no one ever forgets. The first yes is also essential for continuing the journey as an intrapreneur.

Priscila Matta joined Natura in 2007 as a trained anthropologist and her first challenge was to develop an engagement strategy with local communities.[2] This strategy was essential for the sourcing of new ideas to the company's EKOS product line, a pioneer line of cosmetics and fragrances based on Brazilian biodiversity. In particular, she needed to resolve the issue around the Palmeira do Piauá community. Natura had sourced natural ingredients from this community and was successful in its commercialization. In these cases, Brazilian law obliges the company to share benefits with the community, but Natura had yet to establish these practices and the first negative media reports appeared, accusing Natura of taking undue benefit from the exploitation of the resources of the community. Priscila knew that she needed to visit the community to understand their level of organization, to speak to their leaders. She was, however, new to the company and due to the reputational risks involved, her new bosses didn't want to let her go. Priscila remembers:

> I wanted to get to this community to find out what happened and how people were socially and politically organized, but my direct boss said that I could only go there if there was a strategy on how to act. I said that it would be impossible to come up with a strategy without going there, but he would not let me go.[3]

She had to prove herself for more than 13 months before she got the authorization for visiting the community. It was her meeting with the Goddess when she finally arrived in the community and could start to understand how to resolve the issues.

If you are at this stage and got your first yes, you need to do one thing: celebrate with your team and supporters! This is a major milestone on becoming a Corporate Jedi and seeing your project turn into reality.

WEAPONS: NAVIGATING WITHIN THE CORPORATE IMMUNE SYSTEM

As the word "organization" already indicates, companies are organized entities in which employees are "employed" to fulfil tasks which are detailed in their job descriptions. The moment someone turns to be an intrapreneur – this functioning is challenged. The person steps out of her "job description" and takes precious time to work on a project that might or might not create value to the organization. This is when the corporate immune system gets triggered!

You cannot fit in and be a change agent at the same time

Julian Weber, an intrapreneur at BMW and involved in developing the product strategy for electric vehicles, remembers: "the moment you start talking about electric vehicles, you got at least 80% of BMW engineers against you. And it's completely understandable. They have made their careers based on combustion engines."[4] To move forward, he needed the backing of senior management to develop this new stream of business. In fact, we have not seen a single intrapreneur succeed without support from a godmother or godfather in a senior position. The following power-support matrix might help you to identify your sponsors.

This little matrix might help you to navigate the political system of your organization. We have four groups represented:

Sponsors (high power, high support for your cause)

These are the people you need to identify first. They will be your godmothers and godfathers helping your project-youngling grow.

How to identify them? You might want to go through the LinkedIn profiles of the board members and the executive team to find out about their interest in social and environmental causes. What are they writing about? What groups do they participate in? Which people do they follow? Which social and environmental concerns do they have or do they get criticism for?

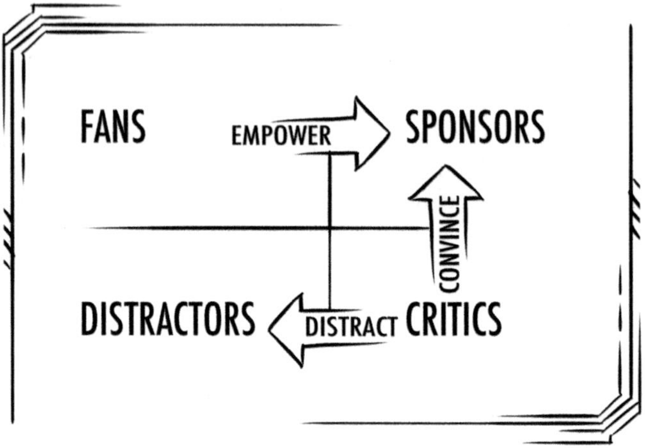

Figure 7.1 Power and Support Matrix

How to engage them? Here's a very important piece of advice from senior Corporate Jedi: "listen first." Before you engage them on your amazing idea, have a starter conversation with them in which you try to find out everything you can on their values, visions, and concerns (see understanding your stakeholder box). Ideally, only on a second or third occasion do you start to bring in your project idea, starting with something like: "what you told me resonated with me . . . I understood that x really concerns you. . . . What do you think if we address x like . . . ?" If you do this, they will feel that the idea was theirs and that you are helping them to achieve their objectives, instead of being "sold" an idea.

How to stay in touch with them? It's important to engage with sponsors on a frequent basis. Send them updates on your progress; ask them for advice and guidance.

An important note on sponsors: you'd better have two or more. A frequent challenge for Corporate Jedi is when sponsors leave the organization. As leadership changes become ever more frequent, make sure you have a couple of sponsors that support your cause.

Critics (high power, low support for your cause)

Next to the sponsors, the critics are the second most important group to identify, because they can kill your project quickly.

How to identify them? They have voiced concern or are actively against your cause and see this as an unnecessary cost or a distraction to the business.

How to engage with them? There are basically two strategic options: first, try to bring them on your side and convince them that your cause is a worthy one. Here you need to work double to understand how this person makes decisions, which people influence their decision-making, what motivates them, and what turns them off. Often, it helps to engage a person that has their trust and understands your cause. The second strategy is to distract them or to fly under the radar. Fly in stealth mode; don't publicly speak about your project but of other things you are working on. When needed create noise about something else, so they think you are busy.

Fans (low power, high support for your cause)

Now here is a group that is frequently undervalued by intrapreneurs – the fans.

How to identify them? These are the people whose eyes light up when they hear about your cause, but you are unsure what to do with this energy and how to take them on board. They are engaged, sometimes in voluntary work, sometimes in specific causes and interest groups.

How to engage with them? Empower them e.g. by giving them little tasks. If the person works in marketing, you might challenge them to see how clients see your cause. If they work in finance, you might ask them to review your business case. Another way to engage them is by providing numbers . . . instead of saying: "I guess our employees are concerned about . . ." you could get numbers: "89% of the people we polled in our department . . ." next to support statements: "Daniela from legal supports this initiative saying it would significantly reduce legal exposure to a new law."[5]

Distractors (low power, low support for your cause)

Those who shout loudest are not always the people you should waste your energy with.

How to identify them? These are the typical nay-sayers. They are against your cause and very vocal about it. You can't miss them!

How to engage with them? Simply don't waste your time. If they have no power and if people of power are not listing to them – simply move forward with your project.

A special note to the HR folks among you: becoming a Corporate Jedi is not for everyone. They need to overcome obstacles, they need to show that they have grit and that they survive a thousand "No's." And this is only a minority fraction of the organization; most of the employees are there to do their job, fulfil their job description. You can lose a lot of motivation and sleep (and money) investing in people who are not intrinsically motivated to become intrapreneurs. In order not to invest into the wrong folks, put out a challenge, make it hard to participate, and then work with the few who have shown that they are really up for it. These are the new leaders of the organization and, most likely, your investment in them will pay off, because they endure as their motivation comes from the inside.

Box 7.1 Understanding your stakeholders

Here are some questions to get you started on finding out more about your stakeholders:

Personality

- Which are the personality traits to the person? Extroverted or introverted, open or closed, curious or expert, self-reflective or not?
- What does the person value? Material or idealistic things, science, religion, family . . .
- How does the person make decisions? Based on data, based on gut-feelings, based on experience. . . .
- What is their personal context? Is he married, does she have children, elderly parents to care for, upcoming retirement. . . .

- What are the person's professional objectives? Become VP, board member, which KPIs must they meet. . . .
- What are the person's dreams? If they had a year off, what would they do? What's on their bucket list?
- What were the greatest achievements? What is the person most proud of?
- Who are the people this person trusts and relates to? Whom do they consult with and why?

How does the stakeholder relate to the topic?

- How does your cause relate to the person's personal and professional objectives?
- Is the person knowledgeable about the topic?
- Whom would the person trust about this topic?
- Which feelings does the topic cause the person to experience?

How does this stakeholder view you?

- Are you trustworthy? Did you prove yourself to the organization?
- Are you competent? Do you have the necessary skills? Or do you have the right team members?
- How does she judge your values?
- What assumptions does the person make about your true motivations?

MEET YOUR JEDI MASTER: PRISCILA MATTA

The relationship between nature and culture always fascinated Priscila Matta.[6] As an early anthropologist, she discovered the world of traditional communities and decided she would dedicate herself to academic research and practice in the field. After 10 years working for different NGOs and researching in remote communities across Brazil, she decided to take a new professional challenge. Priscila had joined Natura some months ago and was the new coordinator of relationships with supplier communities, a position that dealt with traditional extractivist communities and small groups of family farms, who supplied natural ingredients as well as traditional knowledge for the prestigious and innovative Ekos product line. Launched in 2000, Natura Ekos is a pioneer line of cosmetics and fragrances and was the company's top market-based initiative in its quest for sustainability. Ekos is built around the idea of appreciating the knowledge of local communities, recognizing their work, collaborating to build a supply chain that allows self-sufficiency, and conserving the natural environment.

Brazilian law requires companies profiting from the access to genetic heritage and associated traditional knowledge to share the benefits obtained with those communities who originally hold such resources. Natura was among first companies to apply this relatively new law to its bioprospecting relationships with local communities. When Natura announced to the community of Palmeira do Piauí that benefits were to be shared as required by new legislation, members decided they preferred to receive those benefits in cash. People started fighting for a share of this money, even if they had not been involved in the production of the buriti oil sample purchased by the company for commercial research purposes in the past. At the same time the media was debating whether Natura was taking advantage of other local communities involved in the bioprospecting processes for the Ekos line, thus posing an additional threat to the company's strong reputation.

As an anthropologist, Priscila was charged with developing a strategy on how to not only share corresponding benefits with the Palmeira do Piauí community but to mainly do that in a way that would foster local development and environmental conservation consistent with Natura's beliefs. Her suggestions on this specific case would inform the way Natura would deal with other supplier communities in the future.

After an intense year of dogged work inside Natura, Priscila was ready to break the stalemate and present her plan to Natura's executive team. Priscila's anthropological skills allowed her to understand different communities – one of them was the community of people working for Natura. She understood that succeeding in this executive meeting meant getting a sign-off for the next steps in designing the real strategy to resolve the distressed relationship with the community of Palmeira do Piauí. In the meeting, however, she needed to demonstrate professionalism and that she had learnt to understand Natura's business as an anthropologist. The strategy presentation she prepared therefore analyzed different business indicators as well as potential scenarios on how both the community and the company would be affected by the case.

She also understood that the lack of knowledge was the main reason for Natura's resistance to move forward on the case: "at the beginning Natura did not know what to do. They had the right values, but no know-how to address this type of issue."[7] So, her presentation needed to show Natura the first practical steps that could be taken to resolve the issue without further putting Natura's business and reputation at stake. With this in mind, she designed her presentation, knowing at the same time that a visit to the community would significantly change the strategy she was presenting.

Once in the community, Priscila's first choice to halt the fight for money was to announce that the money would be distributed to the benefit of the community and not individual members, strengthening the sustainable use of biodiversity and environmental conservation, according to Natura's principles and the Convention on Biological Diversity (CBD):

> My first strategy was to say: there will be no money, but instead benefits in terms of environmental conservation, community building, etc. This eliminated from the process all the people who were only interested in getting some money, so that we could start working with the people who really produced buriti oil and had an interest in fostering the community.[8]

The methodology Priscila developed with Palmeira de Piauí and other communities orients the way Natura relates with more than 58 communities in 2021. In 2023 Priscila is still with Natura. Starting as Community Relationship Coordinator, Priscila had moved up the corporate ladder and has become Senior Sustainability Manager Biodiversity and Amazonas.

Corporate Jedi Insights:

- It's important to read the people in the room and cater to their needs in order to create trust. Only with their trust will you be allowed to advance with your project.
- Sometimes your next move does not make much sense to you, but it does to those around you.
- When dealing with the community, it is essential to find those players who advance the common good (and exclude those that want to enrich themselves).

NOTES

1 Campbell, J. (1949). *The hero with a thousand faces*. Pantheon Books.
2 Grayson, D, McLaren, M., & Spitzeck, H. (2014). *Social intrapreneurism and all that jazz*. Greenleaf.
3 Spitzeck, H., & Alt, E. (2014). Social intrapreneurship at natura. *Emerald Emerging Case Study Series*, *4*(6), 1–21.
4 J. Weber (personal communication, October 18, 2021).
5 Spitzeck, H., & Alt, E. (2014). Social intrapreneurship at Natura. *Emerald Emerging Case Study Series*, *4*(6), 1–21.
6 This chapter has been written based on the case study "Social Intrapreneurshp at Natura" written by Spitzeck, H., & Alt, E. (2014). Social intrapreneurship at natura. *Emerald Emerging Case Study Series*, *4*(6), 1–21; Grayson, D., McLaren, M., & Spitzeck, H. (2014). *Social intrapreneurism and all that jazz*. Greenleaf.
7 Spitzeck, H., & Alt, E. (2014). Social intrapreneurship at Natura. *Emerald Emerging Case Study Series*, *4*(6), 1–21
8 Spitzeck, H., & Alt, E. (2014). Social intrapreneurship at Natura. *Emerald Emerging Case Study Series*, *4*(6), 1–21.

Stage 8

THE WOMAN AS THE TEMPTRESS

Nowadays this stage on the hero's journey sounds like male chauvinism. In Campbell's terms, the temptress is a metaphor to any temptation, be it in form of physical or pleasurable nature, that may cause the hero to stray from his quest. It is one of the tests the hero or heroine needs to pass in which they are offered relief or gratification that does provide short-term pleasure but no long-term purpose. To the contrary – the temptation – often driven by the dark side – is to lure the hero back into the ordinary world, to give him short-term pleasures such as lust, wealth, or fame and convince him to abandon or forget about his quest. Only by refusing the temptation does the hero prove his values and dedication to the higher goals of his journey.

Many sources point to Princess Leia as the temptress for Luke Skywalker. I honestly, don't think so, as Leia is a leader of the resistance; she is Luke's sister and she did never actively tempt Luke in any sense. I agree much more with the interpretation that Luke is tempted by the dark side, to be united again with his

DOI: 10.4324/9781032615080-9

father. Imagine growing up as a little boy on your uncle's farm wondering about the life of your father – he always asked about what kind of father he had. Remember the lines Darth Vader tells him at the beginning of their fight?

> Your destiny lies with me young Skywalker. Obi-Wan has taught you well. You have controlled your fear. Now release your anger. Only your hatred can destroy me. You have only begun to discover your power. Join me and I will complete your training. With our combined power, we can end this destructive conflict and bring order to the galaxy.[1]

In my view, he passes this test of temptation several times with little difficulty. First, in the fight with his father, he quickly resists the temptation to join him and the dark side of the force. Second, when he is invited by the emperor to kill his father, he refuses. Third, even when he is considered a hero by the rebel army, he opts for exile on Ahch-To. Fourth, one of Luke's life-changing moments happens when the dark side takes control of him, and he nearly kills his apprentice Ben – who then turns to the dark side as Kylo Ren. Fifth, his major fear is always related to the dark side – especially when he recognizes the power within his latest apprentice – Rey.

The stage of the temptress is the stage in which most impact intrapreneurs abandon their first steps and blend back into the system. Early stage intrapreneurs, who are usually younger, especially still have a strong need for belonging. In addition, the system has set incentives to stay within the line. How many colleagues do you know who say things like: "I have a mortgage to pay" or "I still need to repay my student loans" and often opt for a more materialistic lifestyle with fancy cars, apartments, and other gadgets? But also, how many people do you know who are retiring and, without a job in the system, fall into an abyss of senselessness? With their job, they are losing their identity. There are very good arguments to stay within your comfort zone, but there are equally good reasons to get out of the box.

In a recent conversation with Emmanuel Faber, ex-CEO of Danone, he challenged impact intrapreneurs implicitly to resist the temptress. He asked: "how much risk are you prepared to take? You are bigger than your job! Are you prepared to lose it?"[2] He lost his job in early 2021 at least partly because he is a changemaker, because he sees things differently.

There is an important message here especially for early stage intrapreneurs. Milana Momcilovic at the League of Intrapreneurs had learnt this lesson the hard way early in her career: you cannot be a changemaker and belong to the system at the same time. If you step out and do something different, the system either tries to lure you back in or attacks you for stepping out of your boundaries. So, if you are an early-stage impact intrapreneur be prepared! The following words by Peace Nobel laureate Mahatma Gandhi might help you in this regard:

> First, they ignore you,
> then they laugh at you,
> then they fight you,
> then you win.[3]

You are at this stage when you advance on your intrapreneurial journey but suddenly feel attracted again by your career and material gain to an extent, which kills your fire for social and environmental justice. Maya Mehta keeps a picture of 15 orphan girls on her desk to always remind her who she is really working for.

MEET YOUR JEDI MASTER: PAULO BONEFF

Twenty-eight million Brazilian families or one of four people in Latin America are living in precarious housing conditions. Mould and infiltration cause respiratory diseases which count for 25% of hospitalizations in Brazil. Children living in these conditions are less healthy and consequently more often out of school, maintaining a vicious circle of poor health, poor education, and poverty. Houses in the lower income areas – the so-called favelas – are often self-constructed using basically three key ingredients: bricks, cement, and steel.

In 2021, Brazilian steel-maker Gerdau was celebrating its 120th birthday. A perfect opportunity for Paulo Boneff, Global Head of Social Responsibility, to suggest "Reforma que Transforma" (Renovations that Transform) – a project that aims to renovate 13,000 homes benefiting 50,000 people by 2031. The board approved the idea and donated a ten-year budget of more than BRL 40 million. The money is used for donating and financing home renovations within a blended-finance model. Lower income families who can afford small loans will repay their debt, thus permitting others to benefit from the model. Local workers will execute the reforms using local suppliers, thus stimulating local economic development. The business case rests upon three pillars: brand building, strengthening relationships with local governments next to other partners in the value chain, and talent attraction.

Being an intrapreneur, Paulo experienced the importance of the right organizational environment. Supporting projects such as Reforma que Transforma requires leaders that embark on an innovation journey which is already difficult but complicated additionally by integrating social and environmental considerations. He was asking himself: how can a culture that integrates ESG/sustainability and innovation be institutionalized? The moment was right as Gerdau was in the process of transforming itself from a family-led company to a business-led corporation, appointing the first CEO not being a family member, Gustavo Werneck, in 2018.

Working as a catalyst for culture change, Paulo convinced the CEO and the board to embark on a certification process for becoming a certified B Corporation. His main argument: the global steel market was relatively reactive toward new ESG requirements, focusing only on climate change. Going through the B Impact Assessment would provide Gerdau with a benchmark exercise based on high internationally standards (e.g. such as measuring emissions using the methodology by the Carbon Disclosure Project or work standards by following guidelines of the International Labour Organization) and generate a roadmap for the future. The company already had several advanced practices in place and the exercise helped them to already certify parts of the business as B Corp – a first within the global steel making industry.

However, when the board took the decision to go through the B Impact Assessment, he wasn't 100% sure if it would work, how long it would take, and how much it might cost. Afterwards, Paulo was asked: how did you get them to do this?

It seems that the board understood that the exercise would generate a clear roadmap for the company to differentiate on the market as a sustainability leader. Also, Paulo made sure that the process would only advance projects that make sense to the business. Here are his four main recommendations for other catalysts, who are trying to change the culture of their organization.

Build alliances

To implement the B Corp certification journey Paulo did not create a separate area – he built a squad comprised of seven areas including parts of the business, some of which were initially against the certification idea. This helped him overcome resistance and make sure that every area had ownership and was committed to finish the journey together. An important piece of advice is not to hire consultancies! It was crucial to sit down with every business that was going through the certification process, line by line of the requirements – discovering how to meet certification standards in a way that makes sense to the business.

You need a powerful sponsor

Paulo is very aware that without the support of the CEO, Gustavo Werneck, this project would not have advanced. Gustavo stood up in critical moments and was taking risks and advising on how to engage the rest of the organization. Of course, it did not hurt that Paulo developed relationships with the Gerdau Johannpeter family and board members.

Patience and resilience

The initial 18 months after embarking on the journey felt like a "dark tunnel" for Paulo, because there were no clear deadlines, deliverables, and responsibilities, something very hard for an organization used to project management and clear processes. In these moments, you need to be patient and have resilience, as you will have a lot of questions with no responses, while your colleagues will demand signs of progress. This situation leads us also to the final recommendation.

Expectation management

During the "dark tunnel" times it is important to ask your leadership for patience and manage their expectations. Paulo often asked for time and patience, saying e.g.: "give me two months and I'll be back with a recommendation."[4] This provided time to collect data, take benchmarks, have conversations, visit locations, and finally deliver sound advice. It's normal not to have all the answers in the first place.

Corporate Jedi Insights:

- There are two types of intrapreneurs: 1 – intrapreneurs in a strong sense as they develop new processes, products, services, and business models, such as the "Reforma que Transforma" project. 2 – those who work on the organizational culture, acting as catalysts for providing a better corporate environment for all intrapreneurs within the organization. In pushing forward the B Corp certification, Paulo provided a more fertile ground for other impact intrapreneurs.
- A passage of leadership – in Gerdau's case the transformation of a family business into a purpose-driven business managed by executives – provides an excellent window of opportunity. In times when companies reflect on their purpose and are driven by inspiring leaders it's much easier to bring in suggestions such as a B Corp certification and model the organizational culture and structures for the years to come.
- The art of conversations: building alliances, guaranteeing support from senior leaders, building internal alliances, gathering information from the market . . . all this requires listening skills, understanding different stakeholders, and communicating at the right time, the right place, and with the right people in the room.

ON CORPORATE SITH LORDS

Sith Lords are leading by fear. Remember Yoda saying: "fear is the path to the dark side. Fear leads to anger. Anger leads to hate. Hate leads to suffering."[5] The leadership style of Corporate Sith Lords is based on fear because it nourishes the dark side.

One way of spreading fear is firing people who speak up. *Rolling Stone* magazine published an article on 9 February 2023 entitled: "Elon Musk is reportedly firing people over his own flop tweets." Musk convened a meeting asking his staff why his tweets were getting less attention. One of his two remaining top engineers answered based on the data he analyzed that the "public interest in his antics is waning." Musk's short answer was: "you're fired, you're fired."[6]

This in turn creates a climate in which people fear speaking truth to power. It also divides staff – everyone is either a friend or an enemy. Friends support the leader's decision, no matter how irrational they might be. Enemies need to be eliminated or put into their squares. As leaders never really trust even their friends, they aim to collect any information which might compromise the person's integrity and try to lure them into borderline – if not illicit – behaviour. Once something illicit or very private is known about their team members, they have what they need in order to use fear as a management instrument. You are dependent on the health insurance for your sick partner? Great – so work more because otherwise I'll fire you and you'll lose the benefits. You had an affair with someone from the company? Do as I please, or I let everybody know.

As Corporate Sith Lords consider themselves natural leaders, they don't listen, make decisions by themselves, and give orders to their teams. Their communication style is unidirectional. As they are not open to feedback and always know better, they are uncoachable. They don't care about relationships and are 100% task oriented. Successes are theirs; failure is often randomly attributed to some team member who has to take responsibility and live with the consequences.

In the end, this conduct turns their team against them. One prominent example from the Star Wars universe is General Hux in the "Rise of Skywalker." He helps Finn, Poe, and Chewbacca to escape. Finn asks him: "why are you helping us?" upon which he responds: "I don't care if you win, I need Kylo Ren to lose."[7]

Fear creates toxic cultures which seem much more commonplace that you might imagine. Research by Gallup on employee engagement in 2022 shows that only 32% of employees feel engaged – meaning that they are involved in, enthusiastic about, and committed to their work and workplace. Fifty percent are disengaged and 18% are actively disengaged, meaning that they boycott their employer at work.[8] The group of actively disengaged people was rising by two percentage points each year since 2020. It is of little surprise then that many people are dissatisfied with their jobs and might look for something else.

The great resignation describes a historic high of voluntary dismissals – according to research published in the MIT Sloan Management Review – between April and September of 2021, more than 24 million Americans quit their jobs.[9] The top predictor for high employee turnover? A toxic corporate culture! Toxic behaviour such as disrespecting employees and unethical conduct was ten times more important than compensation.

Now be careful young apprentice: we quickly label people to be Corporate Sith Lords. We always have to remember – nobody is ever completely lost to the dark side. Not even Darth Vader or Kylo Ren! If you label someone as the enemy, you easily are prey to anger. Anger leads to hate and hate leads to the dark side.

JEDI PHILOSOPHY: KNOW WHEN TO LEAVE A BATTLE

> Your work is going to fill a large part of your life, and the only way to be truly satisfied is to do what you believe is great work. And the only way to do great work is to love what you do. If you haven't found it yet, keep looking. Don't settle.
>
> Steve Jobs (Stanford Commencement Address)[10]

> Be willing to lose a battle in order to win a war.
>
> H. Jackson Brown Jr. – American Author[11]

"Don't settle," says Steve Jobs, keep looking. For impact intrapreneurs sometimes this means leaving an organization, because it does not want to be used as a platform for change. The question is not if it's okay to retreat – but when. Military personnel speak of tactical withdrawal when it's not possible to hold a position. If your organization makes it impossible for you to live your values at work, you tried to change the situation, but your efforts have been in vain, it's okay to retreat. Think of Finn, who deserted the First Order as they were killing defenceless people. Well, there are Finns in the real world.

On the 14 March 2012, Greg Smith published a very personal piece in the *New York Times* entitled: "Why I am leaving Goldman Sachs." He had started 12 years earlier as a Stanford summer intern, had international experiences, and learnt a lot along the years. He holds that the company's culture "was the secret sauce that made this place great and allowed us to earn our clients' trust for 143 years" but continued that "the environment now is as toxic and destructive as I have ever seen it."[12] According to Smith, the company executes "axes" persuading clients to buy products they wanted to get rid of and went to "hunt Elephants," getting clients to trade whatever brought the highest profit. Goldman Sachs approached clients to "make the most money off of them," and five different managing directors called clients "muppets."

The follow-up NYT publication "A Tell-All on Goldman has little worth telling," published on 19 October 2012, however, points out some issues. Greg Smith apparently never did try to change corporate culture. This is not to defend Goldman, but to outline that you need to do hard work before you leave. You need to show that you worked to keep the original values alive (just as Jo da Silva did at Arup International), you tried to set up products and services that generate value for clients (just as Ana Goffredo and Gabriela Ottoboni did at Sicredi), and you searched for allies within the business. However, when the following conditions are met, you better leave:

- Most of your efforts have been in vain and you feel it's nearly impossible to move forward.
- A new leadership team comes in, changing the course of strategy toward the dark side.
- You are starting to have psychological or even physical health issues.

Of course, timing is important. You leave too early and carry on a feeling of "I should have tried . . .". You leave too late and face serious health issues.

Campbell already mentioned the psychological impact of operating within a skewed system, as he explains in episode one of the Bill Moyers interviews:

> If the person does not listen to the demands of her spiritual and heart life, and insists on a certain program, you gonna have a schizophrenic crack up. The person has put itself off center, he has aligned himself with a programmatic life, and it's not the one the body is interested in at all. The world is full of people who have stopped listening to themselves. In my life I had many opportunities to commit myself to a system and to go with it and to obey its requirements and I would not submit.[13]

In these circumstances, the light side of the force is better off if you start to serve in a different environment, where your energy is put to better use. Resilience is important, but knowing when to abandon a lost fight is also important. Remember Steve Jobs: "the only way to do great work is to love what you do."[14] Campbell agrees: "follow your bliss and don't be afraid. The doors will open where you had no idea that they were going to be."[15]

The following book is classical reading in case you want to know more on when to leave a battle in order to win the war:

- Tzu, Sun (2010): *The Art of War.* Capstone Classics, Capstone Publishing, Chichester, England.

WEAPON: IKIGAI OR KNOW THYSELF

When Rey finally encounters Luke Skywalker on Ahch-To and she walks into the sacred Jedi temple tree he asks her three times: who are you? First time she says: "I know this place." Second time: "the resistance sent me." Upon which Luke says: "they sent you. What's special about you?" and goes on "why are **YOU** here?" She answers: "something inside me has always been there, but now it's awake and I am afraid! I don't know what it is or what to do with it and I need help!"[16] Here Luke answers: "you need a teacher."[17]

The question goes way back to Socrates, who answered to the challenge to sum up all philosophical commandments with "know thyself."

> If you know the enemy and know yourself, you need not fear the result of a hundred battles. If you know yourself but not the enemy, for every victory gained you will also suffer a defeat. If you know neither the enemy nor yourself, you will succumb in every battle.[18]

These questions: *who are you* and *why are you here?* hit each and every Corporate Jedi. At the beginning it's just a feeling, just as Rey says: *something inside me.* Impact intrapreneurs have a feeling that business can be used for the common good. They are afraid, because in their experience, business is used in most organizations for the wrong purpose. And they don't know what to do about it.

As Corporate Jedi continue their journey, they find themselves and begin to articulate a clearer answer to the question – why am I here? Ikigai is a concept which can help you discover why you are here.

Wikipedia presents Ikigai as a "Japanese concept referring to something that gives a person a sense of purpose, a reason for living."[19] To introduce the concept, I recommend you watch the TED talk by Tim Tamashiro.[20] You'll learn where Ikigai comes from and how it might inspire you to develop a personal mission statement. Ikigai is based on the following four aspects: what you love, what the world needs, what you can be paid for, and what you are good at.

Here are some questions which might help you to explore the Ikigai concept:

Discovering what you love:

- Who inspires you?
- When was the last time you entered in the state of flow (so immersed in an activity that you forgot where you were and how much time passed)?

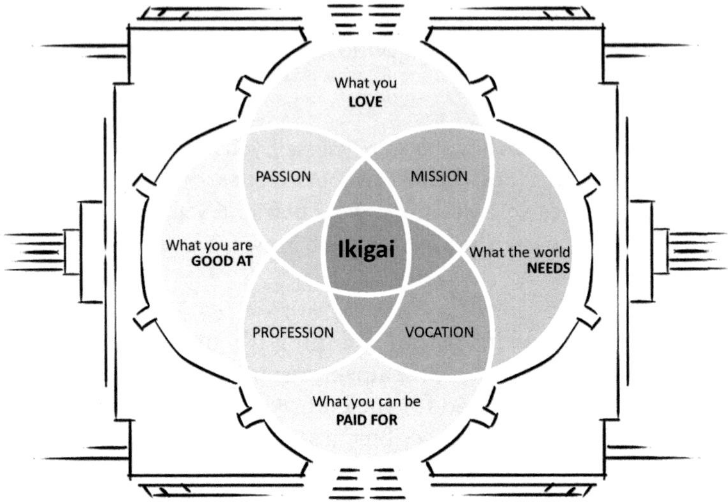

Figure 8.1 Ikigai

Source: Retrieved April 21, 2023, from www.mindtools.com/blog/whats-your-ikigai/

- If you had one year off (maintaining your income and benefits) – what would you do?

Discovering what the world needs:

- How do people express gratitude toward you?
- What would you do if you knew you could not fail?
- If you could write a book that would improve the state of the world and would be a guaranteed success: what would be its title?

Discovering what you could be paid for:

- What is the similarity between your job and your work? Or: which part of your work would you do for free?
- When was the last time you delivered something way beyond expectations? What made you work so hard?

- What do your friends recommend you to do (e.g. you would be a perfect stand-up comedian)? If you don't know, ask five of your friends.

Discovering what you are good at:

- What makes you feel invincible?
- If you could plan your own funeral – what would you like to hear about your life from family, friends, and colleagues?
- What kind of help do people usually ask from you?

Other useful resources for finding your Ikigai:

- "The School of Life – Know Yourself," Retrieved April 16, 2023, from www.theschooloflife.com/article/know-yourself/
- TED Talk on "How to Find Work You Love" by Scott Dinsmore, Retrieved May 15, 2023, from www.ted.com/talks/scott_dinsmore_how_to_find_work_you_love?language=en

NOTES

1 Taken from Kershner, I. (Director), & Lucas, G. (Writer). (1980). *Star wars: Episode V – the empire strikes back* [Film]. 20th Century-Fox.

2 Faber, E. (2021, September 14). Yunus social business. *Unusual Talks: A Fireside Chat with Emmanuel Faber Presented by YSB and BCG* [Video]. YouTube. https://www.youtube.com/watch?v=3wE4nmwRooE

3 Quote attributed to Mahatma Gandhi, see Times of India. (2023, October 2). Mahatma Gandhi´s famous quotes every kid should know. *Times of India*. https://timesofindia.indiatimes.com/life-style/parenting/moments/mahatma-gandhis-famous-quotes-every-kid-should-know/photostory/104100560.cms However, an Associated Press articles casted doubt, if this has been really said, see: Associated Press. (2018, October 5). *Quote wrongly attributed to Mahatma Gandhi*. https://apnews.com/article/archive-fact-checking-2315880316.

4 P. Boneff (personal communication, May 22, 2023).

5 Taken from Lucas, G. (Director). (1999). *Star wars episode I – the Phantom menace* [Film]. 20th Century Fox.

6 Taken from Lucas, G. (Director). (1999). *Star wars episode I – the Phantom menace* [Film]. 20th Century Fox.

[7] Taken from Abrams, J. J. (Director). (2019). *Star wars: Episode IX – the rise of Skywalker* [Film]. Walt Disney Studios.

[8] Gallup. (2023). *State of the global workplace: 2022 report.* https://web.millennium-challenge.com/wp-content/uploads/2023/01/state-of-the-global-workplace-2022-download-1.pdf

[9] D., Sull C., & Zweig, B. (2022, January 11). Toxic culture is driving the great resignation. *MIT Sloan Management Review.* https://sloanreview.mit.edu/article/toxic-culture-is-driving-the-great-resignation/

[10] Jobs, S. (2005, June 12). You´ve got to find what you love, Steve Jobs commencement address. *Standford News.* https://news.stanford.edu/2005/06/12/youve-got-find-love-jobs-says/

[11] Jackson Brown H., Jr. (1991). *Life's little instruction book.* Rutledge Hill Press.

[12] Smith, G. (2012, March 14). Why I am leaving Goldman Sachs. *Financial Times.*

[13] Taken from episode one of the Bill Moyers interviews available at: Lorber, K. (2023, August 23). Joseph Campbell and the Power of the Myth – Ep. 2: "The Hero´s Adventure" [Video]. YouTube. https://www.youtube.com/watch?v=pE8ciMkayVM

[14] Jobs, S. (2005, June 12). You've got to find what you love, Steve Jobs commencement address. *Standford News.* https://news.stanford.edu/2005/06/12/youve-got-find-love-jobs-says/

[15] Taken from episode four of the Bill Moyers interviews available at. Lorber, K. (2023, August 23). *Joseph Campbell and the power of the myth – ep. 4: "Sacrifice and bliss"* [Video]. YouTube. https://www.youtube.com/watch?v=hEqR73j_oMY

[16] Johnson, R. (Director). (2017). *Star wars: Episode VIII – The Last Jedi* [Film]. Walt Disney Studios.

[17] Johnson, R. (Director). (2017). *Star wars: Episode VIII – The Last Jedi* [Film]. Walt Disney Studios.

[18] Tzu, S. (2010). *The art of war.* Capstone Classics. Capstone Publishing.

[19] Ikigai. (2024, January 16). *Wikipedia.* https://en.wikipedia.org/wiki/Ikigai

[20] TED. (2018, September 8). *How to Ikigai | Tim Tamashiro* [Video]. YouTube https://www.youtube.com/watch?v=pk-PcJS2QaU

Stage 9

ATONEMENT WITH THE FATHER

This stage is one of the most important ones, as the hero confronts the reason for his journey, facing what holds the ultimate power in his life. This ultimate power is often embodied as a father figure which needs to be overcome. This is a major turning point in his journey as every prior step has taken the hero here, and every step forward stems from this moment.

In facing this super-power, Campbell writes:

> this requires an abandonment of the attachment to ego itself, and that is what is difficult. One must have faith that the father is merciful, and then a reliance on that mercy . . . only to find, in the end, that the father and mother reflect each other, and are in the essence the same.[1]

The atonement with the father is a central point in the Star Wars saga. Luke, when defeating his father and being invited by the emperor to join the dark side by killing him, answers: "no, I'll never turn to the dark side,"[2] Upon which he is attacked by the

DOI: 10.4324/9781032615080-10

emperor. Luke screams in pain: "Father, please help me." Seeing his son suffering, the all-powerful Darth Vader turns slowly back into Anakin Skywalker, feeling empathy with Luke. Finally, he attacks the emperor and throws him into the abyss. Severely wounded, Anakin says: "Luke, take my mask off."

Luke: "But you'll die."
Anakin: "Nothing can stop that now. Let me once look at you with my own eyes. . . . Now go my son. Leave me."
Luke: "No, you are coming with me. I'll not leave you here. I got to save you."
Anakin: "You already have, Luke. You were right. You were right about me. Tell your sister, you were right."

Those are his last words. The atonement has been achieved. Luke did not want to kill his father and turn to the dark side, thus facing the anger of the emperor. Trusting that Darth Vader can be "turned" back into Anakin Skywalker, Luke completed his quest and destroyed the emperor. He saved his father from dying as Darth Vader, as he died as Anakin Skywalker. In this process, he rises to his own super power, which does not depend anymore on fighting his father or the emperor.

There is a strong similarity here with very senior impact intrapreneurs that have understood that the current leadership team – often represented by the CEO or CFO – are not their "enemies," that there is no black and white between impact and profit but that the two are always interrelated. One of the first persons to understand that business can advance impact is Nobel Peace Prize laureate Muhammad Yunus. Others are the leaders of the thousands of B-Corps all around the world. Today, we also see impact intrapreneurs becoming CEOs or Managing Directors such as Claudia Lorenzo and Pedro Massa at Coca-Cola or Michael Anthony who was Head of Microinsurance at Allianz – precisely because they understand the interactions between business and society. Taciana Abreu at Grupo Soma in Brazil even used a financial roadshow to her favour, when the company was going public and needed to respond to ESG questions asked by investors.

You know you are at this stage if one of your former most powerful and fiercest enemies joins forces. Of course, you need to earn it by believing in the light side in them. Use this support because together little can stop you now, but like all stages in a hero's journey, it will pass.

> The supreme art of war is to subdue the enemy without fighting.[3]

MEET YOUR JEDI MASTER: TACIANA ABREU

Taciana Abreu volunteered for Yunus Social Business in the favelas of Rio de Janeiro, Brazil when she realized that the marketing company she worked for, NBS (short for no bullshit), could channel support for developing vulnerable communities. Following this insight, she embarked on her first intrapreneurial project, launching Rio+Rio[4] – a social business (inspired by Yunus) that builds on the optimistic atmosphere Rio de Janeiro was living in prior to hosting the Soccer World Cup (2014) and the Summer Olympics (2016). Its aim was to engage the private sector in contributing to the development of the city's favelas. The concept was based on a new business model in which favelas gain development work and brand new ideas on how to approach low-income communities. The project attracted support from companies like Nike and Coca-Cola, and all profits made by NBS were reinvested in the communities. NBS even opened an office within the Santa Marta favela. The return of spontaneous media coverage between 2012–2013 exceeded the value of US $1.6 million, an investment return of 213%.

In 2016, Taci became Head of Marketing at FARM Rio – Brazil's beloved fashion and lifestyle brand. After diving deep into the fashion industry's sustainability challenges, such as fast fashion, labour standards in the supply chain, post-consumption waste, etc., she emerged with new intrapreneurial projects. One was "re-farm (reduce, reuse, recycle, rethink),"[5] improving circularity by encouraging consumers to sell their old FARM Rio fashion pieces on Enjoei (a virtual second-hand sales platform). The initiative also included upcycling partnerships so that unused

FARM Rio pieces and textiles could be turned into new pieces. Another project was a partnership with the Yawanawa women from the Brazilian Amazon,[6] using their designs and handicraft to build unique fashion items and providing livelihoods and income for their communities. Taci sees all these projects as a way to "develop relationships, our culture, and telling very diverse stories of Brazil."

When the holding organization, Grupo Soma, was going public and needed support to answer ESG questions from investors, who do you think they invited to be part of the team? After a successful IPO during the pandemic, Taci was promoted to Head of Sustainability at the group level. With the raised money Grupo Soma bought Hering – a very popular fashion brand in Brazil, extending its reach into the production of textiles and doubling its size. Taci loves this new challenge as the bigger the size of the company, the bigger the impact of her work.

Taci is a serial impact intrapreneur and she believes in three things: 1 – as the financial supporter of her daughter she needs a guaranteed salary and benefits; 2 – social and environmental transformations need scale and companies offer just that; 3 – she identifies with corporate hackers[7] and likes to think about how to use the system in favour of positive change.

And – according to her – companies are in dire need of intrapreneurs: "the prosperity of a company depends on its employees getting out of their stagnation and apathy. They need someone who sees a different future, someone who has transformational ambitions."[8]

Corporate Jedi Insights:

- From inspiration to ambition: impact intrapreneurs get inspiration from others and transform it into their own development goals as well as social and/or environmental objectives for their organizations.
- Being an intrapreneur is less risky than being an entrepreneur: as an intrapreneur you have your fixed salary and benefits. However, you need to know how to handle corporate politics.

- Intrapreneurs see career developments as a leverage to scale impact.

MEET REBELLION GENERAL: ENRIQUE PABLO GARCIA

> It's a tough environment for CEOs. Especially for those who want to make a difference, innovate with impact, develop talents and an intrapreneurial culture: in short dodge mediocrity. I do believe that – at the end of the day – impact intrapreneurship generates better results, says Enrique Pablo Garcia, CEO of Klüber Lubrication South America for over 25 years.[9]

Enrique has been a troublemaker for most of his life, challenging his colleagues and bosses to see things differently. He himself says: "I am a born rebel, my preference has always been 'better say sorry than ask for permission.'"[10] For him as a leader this basically means to have courage. Courage to make decisions where you feel that you are right (trust your feelings), but you are afraid. He says: "the feeling of fear is essential" – making decisions where many say: "not sure if my boss will approve," "if this does not work out, I'm toast," or "this is outside corporate rules."[11] This helps him to spot talents as he holds:

> There are only few who ask these questions and say – let's do it anyhow. Most of them stick to the status quo and this is quite understandable as the system is set up to avoid errors. Talents are up against the system and for taking courageous decisions. Leadership in its essence is taking decisions against the corporate current. This is why I try to give my team autonomy with responsibility instead of a command-and-control structure.[12]

To better support talents, Enrique is honing his mentoring skills. He has mentored for the "Unusual Pioneers" programme by Yunus Social Business, Exame's Brazilian Small- and Medium-Sized enterprise programme, as well as Fundación Forge. People under his leadership, I heard say things like: "thank you for teaching me so much," "You are proof for someone who loves what he does," and "I'm always inspired by your leadership."[13] Beyond the positive feedback, intrapreneurial talents from his team in Brazil have grown into global positions. When I asked him: "how did you send your people into corporate headquarters?" he answered: "I didn't. The company found in South America the most critical and scarce resource: talents. Talents who are thriving at taking difficult decisions, talents who attract and develop others."[14]

In fact, this is one of Enrique's main insights:

> I tried to push for change on a global basis, and it did not work out. So, I concentrated on the things under my control, developing intrapreneurial talents. These talents helped to produce superior business results. Soon my international colleagues started to realize: this guy is generating results and developing talents. Then they became curious.[15]

Another of Enrique's insights considers decision-making. He holds that ideally 70% of a company's time and energy should be with current business and operations, 20% with improving the current state of actual business and operations, and 10% should target the future and innovation.

More and more time is consumed by current affairs, which leaves leaders less time to look into the future. He learnt to protect his time and the time of the organization by delegating more and saying "no" more often. Also, he defined clear priorities, as when the company is aligned toward the same objective, it gains a lot of efficiency. "It's essential to focus on those activities which add value to customers." His current motto is: "Serene ambition" – moving forward calmly but consistently.

Corporate Jedi Insights:

- "Trust your feelings" which helps you in making courageous decisions.
- While there are some CEOs who are rightfully criticized, many are looking for help instead. It's easy to critique but not so easy to do better. So, focus on helping your CEO to put better, more sustainable business into practice.

- Focus on things under your control and prove that your way of business is, in fact, better business. If you do, others will automatically get interested and seek your advice and input.
- Intrapreneurs help CEOs with their future agenda and the company they work for to deliver better and more consistent results. Better futures are not shaped following the rules of the past. Creating a better future is about focusing on people, on talents who attract and develop other talents.

CORPORATE JEDI HISTORY – THE GREAT BATTLES

Responsibility Wars, 1960s–2000s

On the night of 2–3 December 1984 the highly toxic gas methyl isocyanate leaked from Union Carbide's chemical factory in Bhopal, India. The official number of immediate deaths was 2,259, next to more than 500,000 injured victims; however, other estimates were much higher. Whatever the precise numbers, it is considered one of the worst industrial disasters in history.[16]

On the 24 March 1989 the Exxon Valdez, an oil super tanker, struck Prince William Sound's Bligh Reef in Alaska, spilling 37,000 tons of crude oil.[17]

In 1995, the British government supported Shell's plans to sink the oil platform "Brent Spar" in deep Atlantic waters. After a campaign by Greenpeace, the company recycled the Brent Spar as a part for new harbour facilities near Stavanger in Norway.[18]

An image showing a 12-year-old Pakistani boy sewing Nike footballs brought the attention of child labour in supply chains to a global public in 1996. The reputational impact forced Nike to use its power to change employment practices for suppliers.[19]

These are just a few examples of major battles of what Corporate Jedi nowadays consider the responsibility wars. Companies were asked to respond to misconduct – training their skills to be able to respond (response-ability) to social and environmental questions. These dark times were characterized by a reactive attitude of corporations regarding the demands of society. Their mindset was most prominently represented by Nobel Prize winning economist, Milton Friedman, who wrote in a *New York Times* article on

13 November 1970 that "there is one and only one social responsibility of business – to use its resources and engage in activities designed to increase its profits so long as it stays within the rules of the game."[20] Today, of course, we know that corporate lobbyists are paid good money to design the rules of the game in favour of business.

In these early years, Jedi mostly operated outside of the corporate realm. The main rebel forces were organizations such as Greenpeace (founded 1971) and WWF (founded 1961) but to a lesser degree also organizations such as the Chemical Industry's Responsible Care Program (a response to Bhopal, founded in 1985) and the Fair Labor Association (response to the Nike case, founded 1999), among many others. Warfare was primarily confrontational and collaborating actors such as WWF were criticized by many Jedi as being too close to the corporate world. The main weapon used by the Rebel Alliance were public media campaigns, which caused reputational crises in the corporate world. The Jedi believed that the corporate world had no potential to foster the common good, a credo which in some battles turned out to be a self-fulfilling prophecy. Today we know that there is good and evil in any corporation (and in NGOs).

The result of the Responsibility Wars was more social and environmental legislation, either on national levels or new industry guidelines such as Responsible Care or labels and certifications such as Forest Stewardship Council. As the belief was that corporations cannot be trusted, some independent third party had to certify that the company was not engaging with the dark side of the force.

The Risk Wars, 2000–2010

The Risk Wars were a natural evolution of the Responsibility Wars. Corporates discovered that it is cheaper to manage risk than it is to manage corporate reputation crises. This gave rise to social and environmental risk assessments, most prominently led by the financial industry. In the end of the 1990s, banks such as Citigroup, ABN Amro, Barclays, and West LB were exposed to criticism regarding financing of projects, which did not adhere to any social and environmental standards. In an act of self-regulation, banks got together and voluntarily adopted the so-called Equator Principles – a set of rules aimed at determining, assessing, and managing social and environmental risks. By implementing the Equator Principles, any big investment project needed to report on its social and environmental implications and contingencies.

As corporate actors are not trusted, the Rebels founded BankTrack, which criticized the Equator Principles for their lack of enforcement. "Who would trust a pack of wolves to self-legislate their access to the hen's barn?" you might ask. During the Risk Wars, however, there was a change in the corporate mindset in so far that at least there was a superficial procedure looking at social and environmental impacts, which some took seriously. Here we saw the first Jedi joining the corporate world, however, with very limited success. This was mostly due to their dominant "NGO" mindset and their lack of business skills. They lacked the language to translate societal concerns into business language and vice-versa. This put many of them in a very uncomfortable position, as their old Jedi friends considered them traitors for joining the corporate world, while their new colleagues always saw them as tree huggers. This first generation of Corporate Jedi, however, followed Corporate Jedi philosophy as they started to believe that corporations can be turned to the light side of the force.

While there were still reputational battles fought in the media, warfare diversified. The focus on risk management allowed the Rebels have an impact on corporate behaviour simply by threatening with campaigns. The conflict between society and companies had already inspired cinema, as evidenced by films such as *Blood Diamonds* exploring how diamonds are used to finance warlords in Africa. Many corporations also stared to engage with stakeholders, as they understood, that they cannot decide **if** but only **how** to engage with stakeholders. If reputation-bashing media campaigns are to be avoided, it might be better to install stakeholder advisory boards to make sure that corporate decision-making respects the views of important stakeholders.

While during the Risk Wars there was more dialogue and engagement, the main spirit of the interaction was still negative.

The aim was to do "less bad" not "more good." Also, the core business model of the corporations was not under consideration. Companies were interested in maintaining business-as-usual by managing social and environmental risks more proactively.

The Business Case Wars, 2010–2020

It was in 2011 that Harvard guru Michael Porter and his colleague Mark Kramer published an article entitled "Creating Shared Value" in the *Harvard Business Review* – basically arguing that sustainability is simply good business. They defined shared value as "policies and operating practices that enhance the competitiveness of a company while simultaneously advancing the economic and social conditions in the communities in which it operates."

The Jedi soon discovered that good behaviour cannot be mandated by laws or industry regulations. So, they were looking for different ways to motivate corporate actors and found the shared value concept very useful in this regard. Indeed, there is a space in which sustainability and profit overlap. The most obvious is cost savings due to efficiencies. The less energy or resources you need, the less you need to pay for it. More sustainable products might also allow one to charge price premiums. Having a good reputation is good for talent attraction and beneficial when entering new markets. Therefore, Corporate Jedi started to use the business case to convince their peers that sustainable business is simply **better business**.

However, some critical Jedi asked: "and if sustainability doesn't enhance the competitiveness? Do we keep plundering the planet?" Another way of framing this issue is asking: what is the difference between your organization and the Mafia? You can't define the difference based on the profit motive, because the Mafia does everything for money – as Professor Rodrigo Zeidan argues in his finance classes: "they just have a different appetite for risk."[21] Just as there is a space in which sustainability and profits align, there is a space in which sustainability comes at a cost. More often than not, this is the space where Corporate Jedi discover if a company takes sustainability seriously and honours its values and principles or goes down the Mafia path.

Again, warfare became more diversified during the Business Case Wars. A great portion was still using campaigns and risk management, but there was a rise in more positive framings, exploring synergies between competitiveness and sustainability.

Social Impact Wars, 2006–2025

Although the seed for social entrepreneurship was planted already in the 1970s, it was only in the early 2000s that the concept took off. The founding father of social entrepreneurship, Muhammad Yunus, started Grameen Bank and gave microcredits to poor women in Bangladesh. In his book *Banker to the Poor* he explains how he uses business as a tool for positive change. His engagement as social entrepreneur at Grameen Bank, which helped millions of Bangladeshis to escape poverty, led to the award of the Peace Nobel Prize in 2006 proving to the world that it is indeed possible to use business as a force for good.

Inspired by Yunus, a new generation of Corporate Jedi emerged. B Lab was founded in 2006 by "three friends who shared a vision to make business a force for good."[22] Benefit Corporations – or B-Corps for short, are legally required to consider the impact of their decisions on all of their stakeholders, not only shareholders. Their bylaws usually explicitly detail their purpose in terms of social and/or environmental value creation. Over and beyond new social entrepreneurs founding new businesses, Yunus also inspired impact intrapreneurs, which were able, e.g., to launch microcredit operations in corporations such as Goldman Sachs, BNP Paribas, Santander, and HSBC – all organizations at the heart of the Capitalist Empire. The very first publication portraying these impact intrapreneurs was SustainAbility's 2008 "The Social Intrapreneur – A Field Guide for Corporate Changemakers."

In contrast to previous Corporate Jedi, this new generation was driven intrinsically. They wanted to show the world that business can be used as a tool for positive impact. This had dramatic consequences. First, business is no longer seen as being a representative of the dark side of the force; it is simply a tool which can be used for the good or the bad – depending on the free will of its leaders. Second, Corporate Jedi were becoming business-savvy in order to use corporations as platforms for positive impact. Third, where these Corporate Jedi were successful, corporations gained a purpose beyond making profit for shareholders. It is still early times, but some argue that turning companies such as Danone into a B-Corp is like turning the Empire's Death Star into a Gaia Creator, a tool for creating new, healthy planets full of life.

At the same time, this new generation of Corporate Jedi is staring at the root of the problem. How do you unleash the intrinsic motivation of executives to foster life? How to deal with the Empire's stormtroopers within corporations? How can you free them? How to fight a Dark Sith Lord sitting in a corporate leadership position with the aim to get richer following a pure focus on profits? Most of the usual weapons are extrinsic motivators that work in one of two ways. Either you act sustainably or you get punished (risk management), or you act sustainably and get rewarded (shared value). This already presupposes that a Corporate Sith needs to be motivated to act sustainably as their natural disposition is egoistic. Sometimes they are no Sith at all, but our own assumptions turn them toward the dark side.

Preparing for Future Wars

Studying history helps us to understand how things have become the way they are today. Identifying patterns in history also allows us to make more solid assumptions about the future.

One thing is for sure: we didn't make it yet. The Capitalist Empire still does not value human rights, environmental protection, social inclusion, the threat of climate change – in short life in all of its forms, as it values money. Scientists all over the globe are ringing alarm bells regarding climate, water, hunger, and other issues that our current system is not dealing with very well. It is therefore understandable that a new emerging class of Jedi is embarking on a more confrontational journey. Fridays for the Future and Extinction Rebellion are seen by some Jedi as Rebel forces that will gain popularity in the coming years.

We humans created this system; only we are capable of changing it. Those of us working as Corporate Jedi need to become smarter and more effective, without losing the humanity we are fighting for – even when dealing with our worst enemies. If Darth Vader and Kylo Ren could be turned, so can our current enemies. Exposing them to acts of humanity, showing that business can be used to produce impact and profit, might spark their own, intrinsic motivation to do the same.

NOTES

1 Campbell, J. (1949). *The hero with a thousand faces.* Pantheon Books.
2 Taken from Marquand, R. (Director), & Lucas, G. (Writer). (1983). *Star wars: Episode VI – return of the Jedi* [Film]. 20th Century-Fox.
3 Tzu, S. (2010). *The art of war.* Capstone Classics. Capstone Publishing.
4 NBS. (2014, May). *Rio+Rio. Ads of the World.* https://www.adsoftheworld.com/campaigns/rio-rio
5 More information about re-farm you find in Portuguese at: Farm. (2024). *Re-farm.* https://www.farmrio.com.br/linhas/jeans-refarm
6 More information about the Yawanawa project can be found in Portuguese at: Farm Rio. (2020, March 4). *Awavena farm yawanawa* [Video]. YouTube. https://www.youtube.com/watch?v=dSjLrUqSpbk
7 Taci was inspired by Clay, A., & Phillips, K. M. (2015). *The misfit economy: Lessons on creativity from pirates, hackers, gangsters and other informal entrepreneurs.* Simon & Schuster. The book has been written by Alexa Clay, one of the authors of Sustainability's "Social Intrapreneurs" publication and co-founder of the League of Intrapreneurs.
8 T. Abreu (personal communication, June 9, 2023).
9 P. Garcia (personal communication, June 27, 2023).
10 P. Garcia (personal communication, June 27, 2023).
11 P. Garcia (personal communication, June 27, 2023).
12 Garcia, E.P. (n.d.). About. Linkedin. Retrieved November 2023, https://www.linkedin.com/in/enrique-pablo-garcia/.
13 P. Garcia (personal communication, June 27, 2023).
14 P. Garcia (personal communication, June 27, 2023).
15 P. Garcia (personal communication, June 27, 2023).
16 Information collected from the following sources: Britannica. (2024). *Bhophal disaster.* https://www.britannica.com/event/Bhopal-disaster; Wikipedia. (2024, February 8). *Bhopal disaster.* https://en.wikipedia.org/wiki/Bhopal_disaster; BBC. (2010, June 7). Bhopal trial: Eight convicted over India gas disaster. *BBC.* http://news.bbc.co.uk/2/hi/south_asia/8725140.stm
17 Information collected from the following sources: Leahy, S. (2019, March 22). Exxon Valdez changed the oil industry forever – but new threats emerge. *National Geographic.* https://www.nationalgeographic.com/environment/article/oil-spills-30-years-after-exxon-valdez/; National Oceanic and Atmospheric Administration – US Department of Commerce (2024, February 5). *Exxon Valdez*

oil spill Prince William Sound Alaska. https://darrp.noaa.gov/oil-spills/exxon-valdez; Britannica. (2024). *Exxon Valez oil spill.* https://www.britannica.com/event/Exxon-Valdez-oil-spill

[18] See McCarthy, M. (1998, November 26). Brent Spar break-up begins. *The Independent.* https://www.independent.co.uk/news/brent-spar-breakup-begins-1187363.html 10- See Zadek, S. (2004, December). The path to corporate responsibility. *Harvard Business Review.* For a chronology of the crisis see Center for Communication and Civic Engagement at the University of Washington, (2000). *Nike chronology.* https://depts.washington.edu/ccce/polcommcampaigns/NikeChronology.htm

[19] See Zadek, S. (2004, December). The path to corporate responsibility. *Harvard Business Review.*

[20] See Friedman, M. (1970). A Friedman doctrine – the social responsibility of business is to increase its profits. *New York Times.* https://www.nytimes.com/1970/09/13/archives/a-friedman-doctrine-the-social-responsibility-of-business-is-to.html

[21] I assisted many of Rodrigo's classes at FDC and recommend following him due to his distinctive style, humor, and expertise in sustainable finance.

[22] Bcorporation. (2024). *FAQs how did the B Corp movement start?* https://www.bcorporation.net/en-us/faqs/how-did-b-corp-movement-start/#:~:text=%20CorpNewsDonate-,FAQs,Corpswerecertifiedin2007

Stage 10

APOTHEOSIS

Apotheosis describes the elevation of someone to divine status; it is the moment of a spiritual rise. The hero becomes god-like. This step begins with the hero's recognition of the divine within himself. Campbell writes: "God is love, that He can be, and is to be, loved, and that all without exception are his children." As god-like the hero overcomes traditional dichotomies between "us" versus "them," "good" versus "bad," even "male" versus "female." Campbell continues:

> If the God is a tribal, racial, national, or sectarian archetype, we are the warriors of his cause; but if he is a lord of the universe itself, we then go forth as knowers to whom *all* men are brothers. And in either case, the childhood parent images and ideas of "good" and "evil" have been surpassed.[1]

Thus, the hero becomes a benevolent regarder of the world.

The dark side nurtures itself from hate, fear, and inaction. In the pivotal moment, Emperor Palpatine invites Luke to join the dark

DOI: 10.4324/9781032615080-11

side and, as he rejects him, aims to kill him. In this moment, Luke entrusts his life to his father's love, despite his being Darth Vader. And love wins. Vader kills the emperor – as his love for his son was stronger than the dark side. God is love. In this moment Luke turns out to be a true Jedi – he won the battle because of love, not hate.

For impact intrapreneurs the moment of apotheosis is when they start to show love, not for the beneficiaries of their projects or the environment but for their "enemies." Young impact intrapreneurs especially see the finance guys or the members of the leadership team who "do not get it" as the enemy. Apotheosis is the realization that there are no enemies.

Valeria Militelli can be regarded a serial impact intrapreneur. During her time at companies such as Cargill, Johnson & Johnson, and Grupo Ultra she frequently implemented impactful innovations. In most cases, her projects motivated colleagues to support her endeavours and join forces. Of course, there were the critics, but she had rarely seen them actively sabotaging her work until the day a benchmarking study she ordered with the help of corporate headquarters never arrived. When she took the effort to call the supplier, they answered: the report was delivered months ago. In this moment, it dawned on her that some of her colleagues were actively withholding the information from her as their lack of support became visible. She felt betrayed and could not understand what was going on. In her anger (Caution! Dark side at work) she complained about the responsible colleagues and hoped that the leadership team would change the workflow in order to avoid this to happen again. Due to internal politics, however, nothing happened.

In cases like this one it is natural to see sabotaging colleagues as the forces of "evil" at work. This changes when the intrapreneur realizes that there are always forces at play trying to convince an organization to move in one or another direction. This is exactly what Valeria did in the end. She started labelling colleagues as supporters, bystanders, and saboteurs. For each group she developed different strategies of engagement, communication, distraction, and workarounds. This brought the issue back to an objective basis and helped Valeria to avoid negative feelings and stress. In the end she was able to implement her project on time, despite the saboteurs! Valeria's case demonstrates that the Apotheosis occurs when the intrapreneur becomes a "benevolent regarder of the world" showing empathy and love to the colleagues, however, without abandoning her fight for life, light, and the common good.

Believe me, you know when you are at this stage. The public will recognize you for your impact, people will come and want to work with you, your case will be written in the next edition of this book. But be aware, the journey is not about you! Stay humble. Focus on your beneficiaries and direct all the energy you are getting toward them.

ON BEING A REBEL IN A CORPORATE ENVIRONMENT

One of the great difficulties for Corporate Jedi is to know when to obey and when to challenge power. Within Star Wars there are many occasions in which young unexperienced rebels do not follow the advice or explicit orders of their leaders. Just think of Luke leaving Dagobah despite Yoda's advice to finish his training. Or – as explained in the chapter on "It doesn't matter if we win, it matters what we fight for" (see Chapter 14 of this book) – the crew around Jyn Erso disobeying the Rebel Council's decision.

Remember the controversy between Poe and Admiral Holdo in *The Last Jedi*? Poe questions the admiral in front of everyone to explain her strategy, upon which she responds: "wasn't it Leia's last official act to demote you for your dreadnought plan? Where we lost our entire bombing fleet." He continues: "Captain, commander you can call me whatever you like, I just want to know what's going on."[2] She answers: "of course you do. I understand. I dealt with many trigger-happy flyboys like you. You're impulsive, dangerous and the last thing we need right now."[3] In the end, she sacrifices herself believing in information she got from him, which does save a small portion of the rebel group. And he got the information disobeying her orders. Without one of them, all the rebels would be dead in space.

So, the clear answer to when to obey and when to disobey is – go and find out. Learn from others how hard you can sail on the wind. It is the nature of the young to challenge the old. It is the nature of the old to give orders to the young. Both think they know best. Innovation against the status-quo. Tradition versus modernity.

If you don't go, you don't know. Don't be afraid. Don't be impressed by all the examples in this book. In a conversation with Lucas Urbano, he remembered one of his mentors saying: "we often see others as greater than they really are, and in contrast, we see ourselves as smaller than we really are." He added: "we are usually the first to create our limits, the journey has more to do with courage and daring than with talent."[4]

There is no way to know your journey before you begin, so failing is natural. Again, Master Yoda gives the final answer in the Last Jedi: "the greatest teacher failure is."[5] So, there are two things you can do: first, you need to make sure, you're learning from past and current mistakes – yours and those of others. Second, your action needs to be motivated by the right values. If you can reference values people share and uphold, your errors might be more easily forgiven.

JEDI PHILOSOPHY: THE GREATEST TEACHER FAILURE IS

> Failure is success in progress.
>
> Albert Einstein (Physics Nobel Prize Winner)[6]

> I have not failed. I've just found 10,000 ways that won't work.
>
> Thomas A. Edison (inventor of the light bulb)[7]

While many famous people have outlined the importance of failure as a process of learning, executives still love to discuss "best case" examples and often neglect the power of failure. Remember Yoda saying, "The greatest teacher failure is."[8]

Five entrepreneur friends got together in Mexico City on a Friday night in 2012 for some Mezcals and decided: "we heard enough about success." Then each of them shared a story about failed projects, such as a business partner running away with the money, a flopped product, etc. The conversation turned out to be so inspiring that they decided to do it again. The meetings turned into a happening, and as they all were entrepreneurs, they founded "Fuckup Nights"![9] This turned into a global movement and in 2023 Fuckup Nights happen in about 300 cities across 90 countries.

Sharing stories of failure can be liberating, fun, and a learning experience for everyone. The Smithsonian listed seven epic fails by Thomas A. Edison – one of them is the automatic vote recorder.[10] Edison thought that the device would "save several hours of public time" and that "my fortune was made." However, when he took the vote recorder to Washington, political leaders said: "forget it." They feared it would influence vote trading and manoeuvring in the legislative process. J.K. Rowling was rejected by 12 publishing houses before one agreed to publish Harry Potter, which sold more than 120 million copies.

Just like entrepreneurs, successful intrapreneurs learn from their mistakes and therefore it is so important to share their failures. Sharing helps to see failure as a "not yet" and invites others to draw on lessons, which can help to advance the cause. So, share your failures, learn from them, and keep going.

> Anyone who has never made a mistake has never tried anything new.
> Albert Einstein[11]

MEET YOUR JEDI MASTER: CARLA CRIPPA

It was in 2016 when Evelin Giometti challenged Carla Crippa and her employer Ambev to join Yunus Social Business Corporate Action Tank and to set up a social business within the company. Ambev, a Brazilian brewing company whose name translates to "Beverage Company of the Americas," merged into Anheuser-Busch InBev – representing beers such as Stella Artois and drinks such as Guaraná Antarctica. Sales in 2021 stood at BRL 72.85 billion. The company dreams "big to create a future with more cheers."[12]

Being a curious character, Carla followed the invitation to find out more about social businesses and its relevance for the company. Together with a group of intrapreneurs, Carla co-created AMA – the company's first line of mineral water as a not-for-loss business, as all profit is directed toward financing projects supporting 35 million Brazilians who did not have access to potable water. She remembers that convincing her CEO was relatively easy, as the company was challenged by the question: how can we sell drinks into low-income communities living in the dry

North-Eastern part of Brazil, who do not even have access to clean drinking water? By slide two of their pitch, the CEO stopped them in their tracks and said: "I got it. Cool idea. Let's do this."[13]

From that moment on started a roller-coaster ride for Carla and her team. Within six months, they took to project from paper into the market – a record time for the company. One and a half years later she remarked: "what I learnt during the last months of AMA would have taken me 10 years otherwise. I have never seen a Profit & Loss statement before, let alone planning a marketing campaign for a social business."[14]

You can track the impact of AMA online. On www.ambev.com.br/ama you'll find a profit-meter showing how much profit is directed toward projects that bring clean drinking water to people. Until April 2023 more than BRL 7 million had been raised, benefitting more than 600,000 people. The goal is to reach 1 million Brazilians by 2025. As AMA finances its own maintaining costs, it is neutral to the company's expenses, essential for not being cut and perceived as a burden on budgets.

One of her WOW moments was when they opened a freshly installed water tube in a community: an elderly man let the fresh water shower over his head. Wondering why he was not drinking the water, the man replied: "I have never had a shower in my whole life. For more than 60 years, I have washed myself with a bucket."[14]

The project didn't harm Carla's career either. While in 2016 she was Sustainability Manager, in 2017 she was promoted to Director of Sustainability and Communications and, upon coming back from maternity leave in 2020, to Vice-President Corporate Affairs and Positive Impact South America.

Reflecting on her role as an intrapreneur Carla asked herself: "which impact would I cause as a social entrepreneur opening my own business, compared to act as an intrapreneur at Ambev, using its immense structures as a leverage for a much bigger impact?"[14] This is also reflected on her LinkedIn page where she presents herself thus: "my purpose is to create ever more positive impact on society."[14]

Her challenge to you? "Try to answer the question: what is the role of your company in society today? What does it do best? If you can channel what the company does best to create impact, your leverage is huge."[14]

Corporate Jedi Insights:

- Intrapreneurs can and do leverage a company's resources, structures, and competencies to create positive impact.
- Acting as an intrapreneur can accelerate your career and improve your visibility internally and externally.

NOTES

[1] Campbell, J. (1949). *The hero with a thousand faces.* Pantheon Books.
[2] Johnson, R. (Director). (2017). *Star wars: Episode VIII – The Last Jedi* [Film]. Walt Disney Studios.
[3] Johnson, R. (Director). (2017). *Star wars: Episode VIII – The Last Jedi* [Film]. Walt Disney Studios.
[4] L. Urbano (personal communication, January 29, 2023).
[5] Johnson, R. (Director). (2017). *Star wars: Episode VIII – The Last Jedi* [Film]. Walt Disney Studios.
[6] Lontos Leonidou, A. (2021, September 28). Failure is success in progress. *Medium.* https://medium.com/@alexislontos/failure-is-success-in-progress-d5b65036e165
[7] Hendry, E. R. (2013, November 20). 7 epic fails brought to you by the genius mind of Thomas Edison. *The Smithsonian Magazine.* https://www.smith-sonianmag.com/innovation/7-epic-fails-brought-to-you-by-the-genius-mind-of-thomas-edison-180947786/
[8] Johnson, R. (Director). (2017). *Star wars: Episode VIII – The Last Jedi* [Film]. Walt Disney Studios.
[9] You´ll find more information on fuckupnights.com. And here is a really good video explaining how it all came about: Fric Animation. (2015, April 22). *Fuckup nights* [Video]. YouTube. https://www.youtube.com/watch?v=NNIl7Lm36HE&rco=1
[10] Hendry, E. R. (2013, November 20). 7 epic fails brought to you by the genius mind of Thomas Edison. *The Smithsonian Magazine.* https://www.smith sonianmag.com/innovation/7-epic-fails-brought-to-you-by-the-genius-mind-of-thomas-edison-180947786/
[11] Quote Investigator (2014, December 16). The person who never makes a mistake will never make anything new. *Quote Investigator.* https://quoteinvestigator.com/2014/12/16/no-mistakes/
[12] Taken from the corporate website, which can be found here: ABInBev. (2024). *Our purpose we dream big to create a future with more cheers.* https://www.ab-inbev.com/who-we-are/our-purpose/
[13] C. Crippa (personal communication, May 11, 2023).
[14] Cited by C. Crippa (personal communication, May 11, 2023).

Stage 11

THE ULTIMATE BOON

In Campbell's hero's journey, the ultimate boon is the final stage of initiation. It is the moment the hero achieves the goal of the quest. All the tests and challenges the hero needed to pass through were necessary to show that the hero is worthy of the boon as "its guardians dare release it only to the duly proven." Using everything he learnt on the journey, he overcomes all tests and obstacles.

"Trust your feelings" is a recommendation Luke Skywalker got a lot of times. He learnt that using the light side of the force, fuelled by love and life, is more powerful in the end. As the emperor and Darth Vader are gone, the empire has been finally defeated and peace returns to the galaxy. Luke has been "illuminated" and turned into a true Jedi Master. He is now able to rebuild the Jedi order.

For impact intrapreneurs the ultimate boon is the implementation of their world-changing project at scale. For Susie Lonie and Nick Hughes, the ultimate boon might well have been the

DOI: 10.4324/9781032615080-12

implementation and scaling of M-Pesa, a mobile payment system that brought financial inclusion to millions of people in Kenya and beyond.

For Miriam Turner and Nick Hill it probably was the Net-Works project at Interface, which turns old fisher nets found in the ocean into carpet, benefitting coastal communities and sea life. During their journey they have learnt to formulate projects, which create value for society as well as for the companies they worked for. They have become master impact intrapreneurs that inspire and guide others on their quest.

You are at this stage when you were able to implement and scale your project. Your idea has turned into a project, and this project was implemented and is creating value for your organization as well as beneficiaries. Probably you are getting recognition and awards. When intrapreneurs get their ultimate boon, they usually focus on two things: 1 – finding someone who can manage the existing business, and then they start on 2 – start something new. Very seldom do we find intrapreneurs setting up their venture and then simply administering it.

MEET YOUR JEDI MASTERS: MIRIAM TURNER AND NICK HILL

Miriam Turner worked first as Innovation Projects Manager and then Innovations Director EMEAI at Interface – an Atlanta-based world leader in carpets solutions founded by Ray Anderson, a leading thinker on industrial ecology and sustainability. It was in 2012 when she involved her college friend Nick Hill, project manager at the Zoological Society of London (ZSL). Together they started Net-Works, a project aiming to improve living conditions of rural communities by collecting discarded fishing nets and recycling them into nylon yarn, reused in the manufacturing of carpet tile. Nick described why he joined the project like this:

> I am passionate about making marine conservation pro-poor and moving it away from its over-dependence on donor funding. Net-Works

> offered an opportunity to pilot a conservation model that is self-financed at a local level and empowers communities to tackle their own environmental problems.[1]

The damage caused by abandoned fishing nets is devastating for marine life such as tortoises, dolphins, fish, and seabirds alike. Net-Works motivates coastal communities to collect old fishing nets by paying them by weight. In collaboration with the 36 communities in the Philippines and Cameroon they created community banks, giving 1,500 families financial education as well as access to finance and providing a healthier environment to approximately 162,000 people.[2]

It wasn't easy to sell this project internally, as Miriam recounts:

> Internally, I had to demonstrate the value of Net-Works, presenting the business case in different ways to different people, depending on whether I was talking to the CFO or the head of marketing. That's what intrapreneurs do within their organizations – hustle and make the case in different ways to different people. Once you've proven that the concept works, the next challenge is scaling up.[3]

Due to its self-sustaining business model Net-Works operates as an internal social enterprise (or not-for-loss business) which covers its own cost. Any remaining profit goes to the community banks as savings. The programme has also improved brand value as it featured Interface in magazines such as the *Economist* and contributed to over US $23.5 million in sales (based on an investment of less than US $1 million). Eighty-three of Interface's sales team found that Net-Works strengthened relationships with customers.

Of course, the business case is important for getting approval from the company. However, it's not what really motivates intrapreneurs. Miriam reflected:

> The best thing for me is hearing other people talk so enthusiastically about Net-Works: a colleague who says that they told their family about it, or someone at an event who comes over to me and says "I heard about Net-Works and I think it's brilliant." Another moment

> that sticks in my mind is when we won the Ethical Corporation award in 2014 for best business-NGO partnership. I was on maternity leave with new-born twins when I got the news and I felt so proud. Net-Works is like my third baby![4]

Corporate Jedi Insights:

- You need to frame your storytelling according to the person you are talking to. The CFO wants to know about payback and profits, the head of marketing about sales, client satisfaction, and retention.
- Partnering with NGOs and other institutions can get you insights, technical expertise, trust, and access to local communities.
- Sometimes a "not-for loss" business model is sufficient, as it can create spill-over effects on corporate branding and client satisfaction.

HOW TO BUILD A REBEL BASE

When talking to leaders of impact intrapreneurs they usually ask: how to develop a corporate culture that combines ESG and Innovation and creates an enabling environment for impact intrapreneurs? In short: how to build a Rebel Base?

BASF is a multinational chemical company operating in more than 90 countries driven by its purpose to "create chemistry for a sustainable future." It initiated its activities in Brazil in 1911. In 2016, the company started the implementation of a new social engagement strategy based on two pillars: corporate citizenship and shared value. BASF Brazil started to explore the concept of impact intrapreneurship to support this strategy and to develop new shared value initiatives. In 2018, BASF co-founded the Center for Intrapreneurship at FDC together with companies such as Nestlé, Natura, Gerdau, Vedacit, Klüber Lubrications, and VLI.

During the last five years we developed the following model in intensive discussions with Cristiana Xavier de Brito (Corporate Affairs and Sustainability Director), Caroline Lima (Corporate

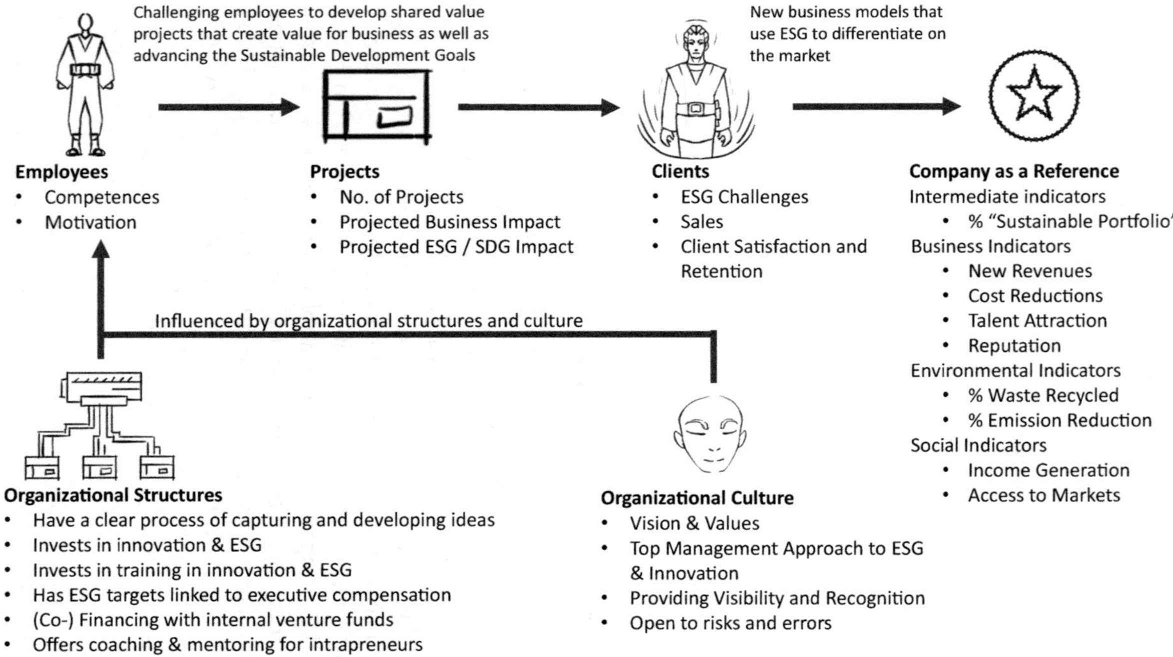

Figure 11.1 Constructing a rebel base – toward an impact intrapreneurial culture

Sustainability Manager), Ivania Palmeira (Social Management Consultant), and Rodolfo Walder Viana (Senior Sustainability Manager).

It all starts challenging employees to develop new and more sustainable processes, products, services, and business models. To support these intrapreneurs, we developed an online course which introduces the concept of impact intrapreneurship, supports participants in developing ideas, and turns these ideas into viable projects. The final deliverable of the online course is a five-minute video pitch in which participants explain the project, how it creates value for business, and how it advances the company's ESG agenda.

The pitches are evaluated by their contribution to business and addressing ESG priorities of the company, and the most promising projects get selected for a pre-acceleration phase. In this phase the potential intrapreneurs get support from mentors and further training, so they design their perfect pitch to the leadership team. During the Demo Day participants get the opportunity to pitch to senior leaders, who decide if the project gets implemented.

Ideally, these projects create value for clients and provide solutions to their ESG challenges, thus leading to an increase in sales, client satisfaction, and retention. It helps the company to increase the percentage of sustainable solutions within its product and service portfolio. Creating value for clients helps the company to differentiate on the market – and following the rationale of Michael Porter and Mark Kramer in their seminal article "Creating Shared Value" published by *Harvard Business Review* – provides competitive advantages for the company, such as:

- New revenues from sustainable products, services, and business models.
- Cost reductions (e.g., by increasing energy efficiency).
- Talent attraction (by providing opportunities for employees to bring their values to work).
- Improved reputation (e.g., by free media coverage and client feedback).

Next to these financial results, shared value projects also generate improved environmental (e.g., reduced emissions, circularity) or social performance (e.g., inclusion, income generation). Here are two examples:

Project: Circulaí
The challenge: due to the production process at client sites not all polyamide input is being processed, leaving approx. 5% of scrap material.
The idea: BASF is collecting the scrap material and re-inserting it into the production process.
The business case: the new recycled product line is expected to create around US $1.5 million in revenues per year.
ESG impact: reduced waste production.

Project: women of all colours
The challenge: women from low-income families are looking for employment opportunities.
The idea: by training and empowering women to work as painters – a traditionally male-dominated area – BASF's Suvinil paint brand could generate new revenues.
The business case: the project helps Suvinil in the re-launch of its brand and competitive positioning. By training women in low-income communities Suvinil follows a bottom-of-the-pyramid approach, generating revenues in previously underserved markets.
ESG impact: women empowerment and reducing inequalities.

Over the years we have seen many shared value projects emerging using this structure. At BASF alone we trained more than 500 employees in ESG, innovation, and intrapreneurship. We received 30+ projects and the implementation rate is > 40%. Projects have generated cost reductions, free media coverage, and new revenues next to contributing to the Sustainable Development Goals, principally SDGs 8 (Decent Work and Economic Growth) and 12 (Responsible Consumption and Production).

However, we also realized that the number and quality of projects depends on the company's investment, structures, and culture. In a benchmarking study using 420 big corporations in Brazil, we found significant performance differences between two groups of companies: those who invest less and have weaker structures in terms of ESG and innovation, and those who invest more and have more solid structures. Companies that invest more, have a structured process to capture and develop ideas, offer coaching and mentoring, provide seed money via internal investment funds, link ESG targets to executive compensation, and have a board committee on ESG have a higher chance to report the following business benefits:

- Improved organizational climate.
- Higher number of suggested and implemented projects.
- Higher revenues from products and services launched during the last three years.
- Higher revenues from certified sustainable products and services.
- Higher client retention rate.
- Reduction in costs due to efficiencies.
- Reduced cost of capital due to access to ESG funding.

On the more cultural side of things, we understood that the vision and values of the company, the top leadership's approach to ESG and innovation, next to recognizing intrapreneurial talent and accepting failure as a part of the learning journey, are essential components of an intrapreneurial culture.

MEET YOUR JEDI MASTER: SANDRA BOCCIA

On the 27 June 2023, the media platform "Um só planeta" (The only planet) won two awards of the International News Media Association and was considered "Best in Latin America."[5] "Um só planeta" bundles sustainability news from across the editorial spectrum of one of the biggest media companies in Brazil – Editora Globo – and has become the place for news on climate change and sustainability. The initiative implemented a series of journalistic innovations: 1 – the way articles are constructed is neither the typical doomsday reporting nor marketing/greenwashing for corporate clients but focusing on solutions and inspiration; 2 – sponsoring companies have a seat on the editorial board, not to influence what gets published but to add depth and industry expertise and to share benchmarks and their vision; 3 – the platform collects ESG insights from across 22 brands of Editora Globo and thus increases their visibility.

The intrapreneur behind the initiative, Sandra Boccia, remembers that it took her and her team a long way to get there. At the beginning people simply ignored her emails or said: "we already have a big portfolio which is difficult to maintain, why launching a new brand?"[6] She traces her resilience back to the entrepreneurial roots of her parents – both entrepreneurs – she knew the ups and downs and how to challenge a "no" from above. Three things were essential to help her convince her organization to move forward: support from the CEO, the business case, and flying under the radar. Let's start with the last.

Flying under the radar – she challenged one of her team members to review what already got published regarding climate change and sustainability within the Globo portfolio of brands and to find out what interest her colleagues had in providing this content more visibility. Understanding her colleagues across the company also helped to create a model that does not depend on creating new "sustainability content," which would have been another barrier for implementation.

The business case – learning from start-up financing she looked for investors that did not just bring the money but also expertise. Engaging them in an editorial board, they are involved in discussing content but without inhibiting journalistic independence and freedom. This allowed Sandra to remunerate other Globo brands for their content, plus providing them with a broader viewer base. Consequently, Globo brands have a business interest in publishing on the platform while preserving their readership.

Creating synergies, increasing viewer base, creating a sustainable portfolio and ultimately making more money also convinced the sceptics. "The CEO's engagement and support are essential,"[7] says Sandra.

On the 6 April 2021, in the middle of the pandemic, "Um só planeta" went live. Today, the platform attracts more than

2 million pageviews, a very good number for a relatively new platform. Sandra's satisfaction, however, comes less from these numbers than from conversations with colleagues, who say: "I started recycling at home" or friends who report that "I convinced my wife not to buy a diesel car, because of its environmental impact"[8] after reading about it on the platform. The new revenue stream also allowed Sandra and her team to compensate all emissions caused by Editora Globo's print media and events by supporting reforestation projects in Brazil's Mata Atlântica.

Corporate Jedi Insights:

- Instead of simply getting investors, learn from start-ups and bring "smart capital" on board – engage your investors.
- Listening to the needs and challenges of colleagues might help you to construct a solution which adds value to their work, motivating them to collaborate.

And again, the business case is essential to get leadership support.

NOTES

1 M. Turner & N. Hill (personal communication, February 20, 2023).
2 See Heller, C. (2018). Interface net-works. In *The intergalactic design guide.* Island Press. https://link.springer.com/chapter/10.5822/978-1-61091-882-4_8; Economics of Mutuality. (2023). *Interface Inc. Net-works programme.* https://eom.org/content-hub-blog/interface-inc; Slavin, T. (2017, September 8). The impact intrapreneurs – how interface and ZSL collaborated to create net-works. *Reuters Events Sustainable Business.* https://www.reutersevents.com/sustainability/impact-intrapraneurs-how-interface-and-zsl-collaborated-create-net-works.
3 M. Turner & N. Hill (personal communication, February 20, 2023).
4 M. Turner & N. Hill (personal communication, February 20, 2023).
5 McMullan, D. (2023, May 29). *INMA reveals 40 global media awards first-place winners, Bergens Tidende takes top prize.* INMA International News Media Association. https://www.inma.org/blogs/main/post.cfm/inma-reveals-40-global-media-awards-first-place-winners-bergens-tidende-takes-top-prize
6 S. Boccia (personal communication, June 26, 2023).
7 S. Boccia (personal communication, June 26, 2023).
8 S. Boccia (personal communication, June 26, 2023).

Stage 12

REFUSAL OF THE RETURN

The 17 stages of Campbell's hero's journey are divided into three acts: Departure, Initiation and Return. The Refusal of the Return is the first stage of the third act: Return. Campbell writes:

> When the hero quest has been accomplished . . . the adventurer still must return with his life-transmuting trophy. The full round, the norm of the monomyth, requires that the hero shall now begin the labor of bringing the runes of wisdom, the Golden Fleece, or his sleeping princess, back into the kingdom of humanity.[1]

However, leaving the space of the hero's illumination is a rather unpleasant experience and Campbell explains that:

> the responsibility (of going back) has been frequently refused. Even the Buddha, after his triumph, doubted whether the message of realization could be communicated, and saints have been reported to have passed away while in the supernal ecstasy. Numerous indeed

DOI: 10.4324/9781032615080-13

> are the heroes fabled to have taken up residence forever in the blessed isle of the unaging Goddess of Immortal Being.[2]

In fact, illumination cannot be put into words and easily shared with others. This makes going back into the ordinary world challenging – how can you transmit to others that the hero has profoundly changed? In the end, however, the boon is there to benefit the hero's community and possibly the whole world.

Luke Skywalker does not return to the ordinary world after defeating the emperor. He never again set foot on Tatooine, where he grew up with his uncle and aunt. Only Rey, after she won her battle, visits the moisture farm on Tatooine where Luke grew up, buries Luke's and Leia's lightsabers, and, when asked by a local who she is, answers: Rey Skywalker. Instead of returning to the ordinary world, Luke tried to rebuild the Jedi Order. As he failed, he went into exile and needed to be brought back by Rey.

How does an impact intrapreneur go back into the office after implementing a project? Imagine Jo da Silva, an engineer at Arup – a well-known firm constructing world-famous buildings such as the Sydney Opera house.[3] In her spare time, Jo educated herself as a post-disaster engineer. In 2005, after the Indian Ocean earthquake and tsunami, she worked with the United Nations High Commissioner for Refugees, coordinating the construction of over 60,000 shelters in Sri Lanka in just 6 months. Do you think she could simply go back into the Arup office and continue to design beautiful buildings? Of course not! This is why she founded Arup International Development – a specialist business within Arup focusing on solutions for resilience to climate change, rebuilding after disasters, and inclusive cities. By going back to her office, Jo da Silva brought her "Golden Fleece" back into the kingdom of humanity and benefited people in need in many parts of the world.

You are at this stage if you feel a certain lack of attention and enthusiasm for your project. It is natural to enjoy standing in the limelight, but it might be time to go back. Back to where? Back to the ordinary world, not to return to your previous position, but potentially to train other intrapreneurs or to up the game. Ask yourself: where would the universe put me with my network and skills to create positive impact? How can I strengthen the community of corporate rebels teaching others what I know? A perfect opportunity might be acting as a mentor to Corporate Padawans.

JEDI PHILOSOPHY – IT CANNOT BE COMMUNICATED

As we have seen at stage 12, your enlightening is difficult to explain. What is the force you are using? Following starwars.com, the "Force is a mysterious energy field created by life that binds the galaxy together."[4] Very clear, isn't it?

The Force is hard to explain, here are some definitions[5]:

Obi-Wan Kenobi: "an energy field created by all living things."
Luke Skywalker: "The Force is now a power you have. It's not about lifting rocks. It's the energy between all things, a tension, a balance, that binds the universe together."
Darth Vader: "The ability to destroy a planet is insignificant next to the power of the Force."

Here is the explanation from the creator, George Lucas, during a production meeting for *The Empire Strikes Back*:

> The act of living generates a force field, an energy. That energy surrounds us; when we die, that energy joins with all the other energy. There is a giant mass of energy in the universe that has a good side and a bad side. We are part of the Force because we generate the power that make the Force live.[6]

To keep it mysterious, here is a final quote from Ahsoka Tano: "in my experience, when you think you understand the Force, you realize just how little you know."[7]

When do people accept that there is such a thing as the force? When they see it in action. Here are some examples on how you might communicate things that cannot be communicated.

Make them feel the pain

As Brazil implemented a new law on recycling and post-consumption waste, the CEO of a cosmetics company felt that things were not moving fast enough. So, he took the senior leadership to an open waste dump where they could see how children were looking for food in the newly arrived waste, dumped off by the trucks. He asked his team to collect some of the waste and they saw that a part of it was packaging from their own company. Then the CEO said: "Society does no longer accept that we are not taking responsibility for the waste we generate" (extracted from Chatham House Rules). Things were moving much faster after this experience.

Let them see the light

"One of the first things I did was to take the shareholders to know the Vivenda Programme," remembers Tarcila Reis Ursini, independent member of the Strategy, Innovation, and Sustainability Committee at Vedacit – a company producing wall coatings and construction materials.[8] The Vivenda Programme is a social business that reforms houses in low-income communities. Traditionally, the poor build their houses without planning and do not use coating products. Consequently, the houses suffer leakages, mould, and poor ventilation, factors contributing to respiratory diseases, which rank fourth in the National Health Service's list of reasons for hospitalizations. Sammuel Sesti Minutto, Director for Communication of the Sustainable Construction Movement, went straight to the point in an interview: "it is useless to treat the disease without treating the dwelling. If humidity is not eliminated, the patient has no real chance to stay healthy."[9]

During the visit to the Vivenda Programme it became clear that communities did not need mere donations but rather Vedacit products and services to improve the quality of their lives and to protect the health of the people living in the houses. One of the shareholders remembers this crucial moment:

> It was a transformative moment. We got to visit a woman whose house was renovated. Forty per cent of the Brazilian population lives in precarious homes. This is a hard and sad reality. We noticed that our products might make a difference in the lives of these people.[10]

Another shareholder highlights the lessons learned from the visits: "we noticed that we could make a difference and that this would make sense for Vedacit's business. We then decided to create a social price for this low-income population."[11] The social price made Vedacit products available at lower costs while still keeping some margin. The main insight for the shareholding family? The possibility of creating a business model that generates positive impact improves the quality of life in the communities and – at the same time – being financially profitable.

So, if it can't be communicated – show them! Let them feel, smell, and experience the good and the bad of corporate conduct. As their hearts are touched, their minds will open, and they will start looking for new solutions.

MEET YOUR JEDI MASTER: JO DA SILVA (DBE)

Jo da Silva was born in 1967 in Washington, DC. As her father was a diplomat, she learnt to love travel and to connect to local communities from an early age. She studied engineering at the University of Cambridge and after graduating worked in India, building accommodations and water supply systems. India turned out to be a pivotal moment in her life as it sharpened her awareness of the interdependence of humans and their environment.

Inspired by Ove Arup's values that "work is only valuable if it has something higher to strive for"[12] she joined Arup as a graduate engineer. Arup is known for building the Sydney Opera house and being a humane and socially useful organization. Living her passion, Jo got involved with post-disaster relief work, constructing refugee camps in Tanzania in 1994. The camp turned into a new city with nearly 500,000 people, and she could observe human dependence on nature's resources: "I watched the forests walk backwards as people chopped down trees for firewood and saw the water level in the lake go down inch by inch every day, like watching someone drink a glass of water."[13] There it was again, the link between human development and nature.

When one of the board directors was looking for "activists, not corporate animals" to build Arup's Sustainable Task Force, she was one of the first to join. Due to her experience, she was invited by UN Refugee Agency to coordinate post-disaster shelter construction in Sri Lanka – partnering with approx. 100 NGOs they managed to build 60,000 shelters in only 6 months. Here she realized that "I could lead, and that courage, conviction and communication are powerful tools."[14]

All this work inspired her to better use Arup as a platform for positive impact. Supporting the company's mission "to shape a better world," in 2007, she proposed to create Arup International Development as a consultancy business focused on development work. As she says: "there was a need I felt I could fill – and an 'army' of talent in Arup that could be harnessed and redirected."[15] She intentionally framed it as a not-for-profit business unit and not as philanthropic work: "I did not ask Arup for resources. From the outset I was clear that Arup International Development would need to operate as a self-sustainable business."[16]

Arup International Development is today a specialist business within the company. From climate change resilience to disaster relief their team works with city governments, development, and humanitarian organizations. Their partners include Médecins Sans Frontières, UN-Habitat, BRAC, and multilateral banks. The operations achieved scale, and whenever asked to tender competitively, AID seeks to make a surplus to have resources to invest. Jo da Silva sees that "the success of AID is infecting others in the firm to believe that we can do this type of work well without losing money."[17]

In 2023, Jo da Silva is still with Arup serving as Global Director of Sustainable Development as an Officer to the Group Board "promoting excellence and innovation that delivers social outcomes."[18] In 2016 she founded Resilience Shift to improve the resilience of critical infrastructure. Jo da Silva received numerous recognitions for her work: she was made Dame Commander of the British Empire in 2021 and received the Gold Medal of the Institution of Structural Engineers in 2017 for her work on urban resilience.

Corporate Jedi Insights:

- You can leverage the founder's values as well as the company's vision and mission to support your project, as the company needs to demonstrate to external stakeholders how it puts its mission into practice.

- If you are searching for jobs – look out for inspiring visions, missions, and values of the company, together with evidence of how they put these values into practice. In general, make sure that the organizational values fit your own as you'll find other Corporate Jedi working in these environments.
- Activists, not corporate animals, can drive innovation and sustainability within the company.

NOTES

1 Campbell, J. (1949). *The hero with a thousand faces*. Pantheon Books.
2 Campbell, J. (1949). *The hero with a thousand faces*. Pantheon Books.
3 Grayson, D., McLaren, M., & Spitzeck, H. (2014). *Social intrapreneurism and all that jazz*. Greenleaf.
4 Taken from Starwars.com. (2014). *Databank the force*. https://www.starwars.com/databank/the-force
5 Taken from The Force. (2014, January 28). *Wikipedia*. https://en.wikipedia.org/wiki/The_Force; Sherlock, B. (2021, May 31). *Star wars: 15 quotes about the force, ScreenRant*. https://screenrant.com/star-wars-best-quotes-force/
6 The Force. (2024, January 28). *Wikipedia*. https://en.wikipedia.org/wiki/The_Force
7 McGinley, R. (2021, October 2). *Star wars – 5 of Ahsoka Tano's best quotes in the clone wars & her 5 best in rebels, ScreenRant*. https://screenrant.com/star-wars-ahsoka-tano-best-quotes-clone-wars-rebels/
8 Information taken from the e-book published by Arruda, C., Braga, C., Sardenberg, D., Pitta, E., Barcellos, E., Spitzeck, H., & Guimarães, S. (2022). *Inovação o motor do ESG*, especially the case study on Vedacit written by Spitzeck, H., & Alt, E.
9 O impacto das infiltrações e do mofo na saúde, Terra. (2020, May 8). https://www.terra.com.br/noticias/dino/o-impacto-das-infiltracoes-e-do-mofo-na-saude,efc80ef76fd83f4ac85d48b55bf18dfec454876m.html
10 Information taken from the e-book published by Arruda, C., Braga, C., Sardenberg, D., Pitta, E., Barcellos, E., Spitzeck, H., & Guimarães, S. 2022). *Inovação o motor do ESG*, especially the case study on Vedacit written by Spitzeck, H., & Alt, E.
11 Information taken from the e-book published by Arruda, C., Braga, C., Sardenberg, D., Pitta, E., Barcellos, E., Spitzeck, H., & Guimarães, S. (2022). *Inovação o motor do ESG*, especially the case study on Vedacit written by Spitzeck, H., & Alt, E.
12 J. da Silva (personal communication, June 18, 2023).
13 See Nuttall, P. (2022). Engineers build the fabric of society. we need them in government. *The New Statesman*. Retrieved June 15, 2022.
14 J. da Silva (personal communication, June 18, 2023).
15 J. da Silva (personal communication, June 18, 2023).
16 Grayson, D., McLaren, M., & Spitzeck, H. (2014). *Social intrapreneurism and all that jazz* (p. 16). Greenleaf.
17 J. da Silva (personal communication, June 18, 2023).
18 Arup. (2024). *Jo da Silva*. https://www.arup.com/our-firm/jo-da-silva

Stage 13

THE MAGIC FLIGHT

In the hero's journey, Joseph Campbell writes about the magic flight: "if the hero's wish to return to the world has been resented by the gods or demons, then the last stage of the methodological round becomes a lively, often comical, pursuit."[1]

Luke Skywalker knew that his endeavour to train the next generation of Jedi failed miserably. As Luke sensed darkness rising in his nephew Ben, one night he confronted him reaching out with the force. As he says: "it was beyond what I ever imagined. Snoke already turned his heart. He would bring pain, destruction, and death."[2] As he ignites his lightsaber, Ben wakes up and manages to defend himself. Luke survives and recognizes that he failed Ben and the other Padawans. He can't stay and must leave. Luke takes the old Jedi texts and flees to an old Jedi Temple in Ahch-To until most believe that he is either dead or a myth. He had become the Last Jedi.

Emmanuel Faber is a legend for corporate sustainability professionals. He joined Danone in 1997, led the Grameen-Danone partnership in Bangladesh with Peace Nobel Prize Winner

DOI: 10.4324/9781032615080-14

Muhammad Yunus, and became CEO in 2014 and President of the Board in 2017. Under his leadership Danone became a "Entreprise à Mission" – a purpose-driven company whose aim is "bringing health through food to as many people as possible."[3] However, due to business performance issues, minority investors such as Bluebell Capital and Artisan Partners were able to summon a majority on the board to support his sudden dismissal in March 2021. The case was a shock, especially for sustainability activists. France's liberal newspaper Le Monde asked the question everybody had in mind: "are these two objectives, environmental and economic, irreconcilable?"[4] Faber retreated to the Alps, very similar to Luke Skywalker's escape to Ahch-To.

In a certain sense you are at this stage when you are fleeing from the place of enlightenment. Unsure if you should return home, you might search for a place to retreat and recharge. Be aware that your journey is not yet completed.

MEET YOUR JEDI MASTERS: ANA GOFFREDO AND GABRIELA OTTOBONI

Ana Goffredo and Gabriela Ottoboni worked at Sicredi Dexis, a credit cooperative in Brazil. In 2019 they signed up for the "SDG Innovation Accelerator for Young Professionals" programme offered by the UN Global Compact, which in Brazil is executed by Fundação Dom Cabral's Intrapreneurship Center. The programme challenges young talents to develop shared value projects – creating value for the company and contributing to the SDGs at the same time.

Ana and Gabriela's "what if" question was: what if we could offer a financial product that encourages our associates (this is what credit cooperatives call their clients) to install solar panels, produce clean energy, and reduce emissions? The programme helped them to frame their idea and secure support from two sponsors in senior management: Executive Director Rogério Machado and Superintendent David Conchon.

The solution: a credit line dedicated to clean energy production which offers lower cost of capital. Financing solar panels helps associates of the credit cooperative to reduce energy bills and to become less dependent on the public grid. Solar panel providers – also associates of Sicredi Dexis – grow their business. Additionally,

1% of panel sales also goes back into a social fund which supports local development initiatives. A perfect example of a tripe bottom line business, Sicredi Dexis profits from providing credit (financial value); there is a clear reduction of emissions (environmental value), and the project fosters local development (social value).

The idea was born in 2019. By January 2023, Sicredi Dexis financed 4,866 projects, which now generate more than 4 million kw/h per month. The cooperative provided credits of more than BRL 185 million and profited from lower refinancing rates offered by JICA (the Japanese Development Bank) as well as the Interamerican Development Bank (IDB). The highest default rate registered since the beginning of the project was 0.45%. In sum, a very successful new product within the portfolio of Sicredi Dexis.

The project shows the power of uniting business and impact. It's the cooperative's product that fights climate change, not simply a philanthropic donation to charity. This allows scaling, as increasing impact is not dependent on more donor money. The better the business, the better for the climate!

Corporate Jedi Insights:

- It can be very promising for companies to challenge young talents to come up with projects that combine the generation of business value with a contribution to the SDGs.
- The advantage of creating more sustainable products, services, and business models is that they can scale through business. Philanthropic initiatives are always limited by the number of donations that can be raised.
- Climate change is not only a risk; it's also a business opportunity!

NOTES

1 Campbell, J. (1949). *The hero with a thousand faces.* Pantheon Books.
2 Johnson, R. (Director). (2017). *Star wars: Episode VIII – the last Jedi* [Film]. Walt Disney Studios.
3 Danone. (n.d.). *Our mission.* https://www.danone.com/about-danone/we-are-danone.html#MISSION
4 Walt, V. (2021, November 21). A top CEO was ousted after making his company more environmentally conscious – now he´s speaking out. *Time Magazine.*

Stage 14

RESCUE FROM WITHOUT

The first sentences about stage 14 of the hero's journey, the "Rescue from Without," reads: "the hero may have to be brought back from his supernatural adventure by the assistance from without. That is to say, the world may have to come and get him."[1]

Luke went into exile on Ahch-To, but he left a map behind, which was divided into two parts. One part was stored in R2-D2, while the other could be retrieved from Lor San Tekka. In *Episode VII – The Force Awakens*, R2-D2 and BB-8 put the pieces together, allowing Rey to locate Luke – the final scene of the movie shows her returning his lightsaber to him. However, in *Episode VIII – The Last Jedi*, we find out that her welcome is rather cold, and it takes some time to convince Luke to train Rey in the ways of the force. Next to Rey, Luke receives another visitor as Master Yoda appears as a force ghost ending Luke's self-pity by telling him: "the greatest teacher failure is."[2] While Luke does not physically leave Ahch-To, he saves the last rebels and the Jedi order by his actions in the real world.

DOI: 10.4324/9781032615080-15

Just as Luke Skywalker felt that he had failed as a Jedi Master and exiled on Ahch-To, Gib Bulloch crashed under the load of work as a social intrapreneur leading Accenture Development Partnerships, a not-for-loss business within the global Consulting firm Accenture. It was on 26 November 2014 that he was admitted to the Thomson Psychiatric Ward, Glendevon Hospital, Glasgow. In his entertaining book *The Intrapreneur – Confessions of a Corporate* Insurgent he explains his adventures in the ward as well as his journey as an impact intrapreneur at Accenture. Personal resilience has become a mantra for him. Within the League of Intrapreneurs, Gib has become a sort of Jedi Master and after leaving Accenture is now running the Craigberoch Business Decelerator – a place which brings talented individuals from large corporations and non-governmental organizations (NGOs) together with artists, activists, musicians, and people from rural communities around Scotland, to stimulate breakthrough innovation that benefits people and the planet. Glad he found his way back into the real world, combining a retreat (magic flight) with igniting change.

You are at this stage if someone came for you, asking your help, begging you to train them – when you find new ways of using your superpowers to the benefit of others.

MEET YOUR JEDI MASTER: MAYA MEHTA

> The great strong oak was once a little nut that stood its ground.
>
> Unknown author – Words to live by chosen by Maya

It happened on the way to work the same way it happened to Gib Bulloch. A newspaper article captured Maya's attention on her ride on the London tube in 2003. The story reported an honour killing about how a young Asian girl was burnt alive by her family for running away with the man she loved. Maya realized that violence related to forced marriages was not just happening on the other side of the world but on her doorstep in London. She got in touch with a local charity that was fighting domestic violence against Asian women and, together with colleagues at her law firm, set up lunchtime sessions advising women on their options and rights. She remembers: "it had to be lunchtime, so the women could escape their homes and we could escape our desks."[3] News spread like wildfire and soon women were queuing up, just to have their voices heard.

And then Maya discovered the business case. Employees of a large banking client joined the initiative and the conversations that were exchanged after each session "created much deeper bonds than small-talk over drinks at a traditional client event." Ever since then, Maya "learnt to search for answers in the business world whenever such a call for action came."[4] And hey, Maya gets a lot of calls. She has set up initiatives on domestic violence, microfinance, and sustainable finance.

Maya discovered herself an impact intrapreneur, camouflaged in a corporate legal department. For her, an intrapreneur "is not something you decide to become, it's something that's innate. It runs through your veins. It is something that is ignited when you are moved by a social or environmental issue."[5] At the same time, the corporate environment is important, because "the business world has the resources and expertise that gives intrapreneurial initiatives wings to fly – without such infrastructure, our fire will dwindle."[6]

Due to her inspiring work, Maya was invited to become a fellow at the League of Intrapreneurs as well as a member of the BMW Foundation's Responsible Leader network. She discovered more corporate change-makers when she ran a series of events about "Putting the Soul Back into Business" (together with the Harvard Club UK), mobilizing social intrapreneurs to connect with social entrepreneurs across the UK. Meeting all these inspiring people made her wonder: "how many social intrapreneurs are hidden in the corporate world?"[7] We can only guess, but her advice is to set up a "Social Impact Hub" at every organization. Of course, she did just that, together with like-minded colleagues, when she joined BNP Paribas in 2011. Today Maya has a dedicated role as UK Head and Global Co-ordinator of the bank's global Sustainable Finance Legal Practice.

Her first recommendation to intrapreneurs is to remember who you are advocating for. She keeps a picture of 15 little orphan girls on her desk. In challenging moments, the photo reminds her of the importance of her work. Her second advice is to know your flow and listen to your body. Juggling the day job and social intrapreneurial ventures demand a lot of energy and can be all-consuming, but as she says: "you can't be firing on all cylinders all the time."[8] Take time to recharge and foster your resilience.

Corporate Jedi Insights:

- Keep the beneficiary of your work in mind; they ultimately are the source of your power and resilience.
- There are many hidden corporate intrapreneurs even in your organization: discover and empower each other!
- Listen to your body! Many senior intrapreneurs have gone through a phase of burn-out as they struggle to deliver on their change agenda, often juggling another day job. Plan and protect regular time to recharge, decelerate, and disconnect.

CORPORATE JEDI PHILOSOPHY – IT DOES NOT MATTER IF WE WIN, IT MATTERS WHAT WE FIGHT FOR

In the line of Star Wars movies, *Rogue One: A Star Wars Story* basically answers the question: how did the Rebel Alliance get the construction plans of the Death Star, which allowed Luke Skywalker to destroy it? The story follows one of the first female protagonists, Jyn Erso, daughter of Galen Erso, a famous weapon developer who is forced to work for the Empire on the construction of the Death Star. He secretly designs a weakness into the structure of the Death Star and hides it on a construction file called "Stardust" – the very name he called his little daughter when they still lived together. However, the file is stored on Scarif – a heavily armed and protected imperial security complex.

Jyn tries to convince the Alliance Council to send rebel fighters to retrieve the plans from Scarif. The council members are afraid, as the Empire has built something which has immense destructive power, and one of them asks: "what chance do we have?"[9] Upon which Jyn responds: "what chance do we have? The question is which choice do we have. Run, hide, beg for mercy. . . . We need to capture the Death Star plans if there is any hope of destroying it."[10] The same council member continues: "you are asking us to invade an imperial installation based on nothing but hope." Her answer: "rebellions are built on hope."[11] Finally, the council does not support her, but some rebels join her in the quest to retrieve the files even without the council's permission in an act of civil disobedience.[12]

Purely based on hope that they are able to retrieve the files and that those files really offer a weakness to be exploited, the rebels embark on their journey to Scarif using a stolen Imperial ship they name "Rogue One." They succeed in retrieving the file and sending the plans to the Rebel fleet, but all of the rebels deployed to Scarif die in the end. Their death, however, permits hope to endure – not surprisingly *Star Wars: Episode IV* is called *A New Hope*. They fought to not let hope die.

When you find yourself beaten up, disappointed and rejected, remember: it does not matter if you win, but it matters what you fight for.

NOTES

1 Campbell, J. (1949). *The hero with a thousand faces*. Pantheon Books.
2 Johnson, R. (Director). (2017). *Star wars: Episode VIII – The Last Jedi* [Film]. Walt Disney Studios.
3 M. Mehta (personal communication, June 23, 2023).
4 M. Mehta (personal communication, June 23, 2023).
5 M. Mehta (personal communication, June 23, 2023).
6 M. Mehta (personal communication, June 23, 2023).
7 M. Mehta (personal communication, June 23, 2023).
8 M. Mehta (personal communication, June 23, 2023).
9 Edwards, G. (Director). (2016). *Rogue one – a star wars story* [Film]. Lucasfilm Ltd.
10 Edwards, G. (Director). (2016). *Rogue one – a star wars story* [Film]. Lucasfilm Ltd.
11 Edwards, G. (Director). (2016). *Rogue one – a star wars story* [Film]. Lucasfilm Ltd.
12 There is a brilliant text written by German Sociologist Jürgen Habermas on Civil Disobedience. Habermas, J. (1985). Civil disobedience: Litmus test for the democratic constitutional state. *Berkeley Journal of Sociology*, *30*, 95–116.

Stage 15

THE CROSSING OF THE RETURN THRESHOLD

As we have seen in stage 12 – the Refusal of the Return – going back to the real world is in most cases a rather unpleasant experience. Campbell writes:

> The first problem of the returning hero is to accept as real, after an experience of the soul-satisfying vision of fulfillment, the passing joys and sorrows, the banalities, and noisy obscenities of life. Why re-enter such a world? Why attempt to make plausible, or even interesting, to men and women consumed with passion, the experience of transcendental bliss?[1]

There seems to be a contrast between the ordinary world and spiritual experience. At the beginning of "The Crossing of the Return Threshold," Campbell explains:

> The two worlds, the divine and the human, can be pictured only as distinct from each other – different as life and death, as day and night.

DOI: 10.4324/9781032615080-16

> The hero adventures out of the land we know into darkness; there he accomplishes his adventure, or again is simply lost to us, imprisoned, or in danger; and his return is described as a coming back out of that yonder zone.[2]

The hero seems to reach into another dimension and the challenge of going back is like, again in Campbell's words, to "represent on a two-dimensional surface a three-dimensional form."

We know from art – e.g. from the paintings of M.C. Escher, that it is possible to represent a three-dimensional form on a two-dimensional surface. In that same sense Campbell tells us about the essence of myths and symbols: "nevertheless – and here is a great key to the understanding of myth and symbol – the two kingdoms are actually one. The realm of gods is a forgotten dimension of the world we know."[3]

In Star Wars this is very evident. One famous scene is during Luke's attack on the Death Star; he suddenly hears the voice of Obi-Wan Kenobi saying: "use the force, Luke." The force is another dimension to reality, and those who know how to use it have a clear advantage. However, as we experience during Luke's initiation, it is difficult to teach the ways of the force because it is hard to be explained by the words available to us. Luke is taught to "trust his feelings."

And here is the reason for the creation of new stories and myths. As Campbell notes: "the boon brought from the transcendent deep becomes quickly rationalized into nonentity, and the need becomes great for another hero to refresh the world."[4] The stories carry the same messages about feelings such as trust, integrity, love, but as time passes the world demands new stories and heroes. As Lisa Cron entitled her book on storytelling – we are "wired for story."

Therefore, the destiny for the hero's return to the ordinary world in many cases is turning into a teacher. Again, citing Campbell: "how teach again, however, what has been taught correctly and incorrectly learned a thousand thousand times, throughout the millenniums of mankind's folly? That is the hero's ultimate difficult task."[5]

In *Star Wars: Episode VIII - The Last Jedi*, Luke – despite his earlier failure – reluctantly again becomes a Jedi Master and trains Rey. We can see this happening as well to some of the impact intrapreneurs within the League of Intrapreneurs. Gib Bulloch has set up Craigberoch Business Decelerator, building the resilience of another generation of change makers. Justin DeKoszmovszky, once an intrapreneur at companies such as SC Johnson and Puma, teaches at the Cambridge Institute for Sustainability Leadership and acts as a mentor for the Unusual Pioneers Program by Yunus Social Business. They have become the Jedi Masters for the intrapreneur Padawans and Younglings of today.

What are the delights of becoming a Corporate Jedi Master and to teach young Padawans, you might ask? Campbell's response:

> The world is a wasteland. People have the notion of saving the world by shifting things around and changing the rules. Not any world is a living world if it is not alive. The thing is to bring it to life. And the way to bring it to live is to find in your own case where your life is and be alive yourself. . . . The influence of a vital person, vitalizes. . . . That is one of the delights of teaching. . . . To see them come alive is the award of teaching.[6]

From my personal point of view I could not agree more – turning employees into impact intrapreneurs, seeing them grow and come alive, is the most rewarding experience.

> We are what they grow beyond. That is the true burden of all masters.[7]

You know that you are at this stage when you are training your Padawan in the ways of the force. Once you start teaching, you'll gain a whole new depth about your own experience and journey.

MEET YOUR JEDI MASTER: JUSTIN DEKOSZMOVSZKY

At 18 Justin DeKosmovszky wanted to be a forest ranger. However, when he studied natural resources at Cornell, he got interested in business and environmental economics. In his early career Justin worked at SC Johnson in Strategic Sustainability in developing markets, implementing a project called Community Cleaning Services in Nairobi, Kenya. It encouraged the local community to pay some of its members to clean public toilets, using SC Johnson's cleaning products. This meant a healthier environment, income generation for the community, as well as new sales for the company – already in 2005. Justin worked on similar initiatives regarding malaria prevention, small scale farming, and other issues. After SC Johnson, Justin continued his intrapreneurial journey at Puma launching the award-winning InCycle cradle-to-cradle certified collection and finally at Ovo Energy where he launched projects fighting youth homelessness and reducing energy consumption.

In 2017 he founded Archipel&Co in the UK, a company that helps to accelerate the transition to an inclusive and sustainable economy. He turned his acquired superpowers into a service offering as Archipel&Co delivers "insights and support the design, testing and scaling of social innovation and inclusive business solutions."[8] Next to running his company, Justin is Senior Associate at the University of Cambridge Institute for Sustainability Leadership – passing his powers to a next generation of Padawans and driven by the next generation's question: "what did you do to make it better?"

Corporate Jedi Insights:

- Some impact intrapreneurs turn into entrepreneurs but hardly leave the social impact space.
- The skills you acquire as an impact intrapreneur are very valuable and might offer you the chance to offer them as a service to others.

Turing into a teacher is often the way for senior impact intrapreneurs.

NOTES

[1] Campbell, J. (1949). *The hero with a thousand faces.* Pantheon Books.
[2] Campbell, J. (1949). *The hero with a thousand faces.* Pantheon Books.
[3] Campbell, J. (1949). *The hero with a thousand faces.* Pantheon Books.
[4] Campbell, J. (1949). *The hero with a thousand faces.* Pantheon Books.
[5] Campbell, J. (1949). *The hero with a thousand faces.* Pantheon Books.
[6] Taken from episode one of the Bill Moyers interviews available at: Lorber, K. (2023, August 23). *Joseph Campbell and the power of the myth – ep. 2: "The hero's adventure"* [Video]. YouTube. https://www.youtube.com/watch?v=pE8ciMkayVM
[7] Yoda in Johnson, R. (Director). (2017). *Star wars: Episode VIII – the last Jedi* [Film], Walt Disney Studios.
[8] Taken from Justin DeKoszmovszky, J. (n.d.). About. LinkedIn. Retrieved December 2023, from https://www.linkedin.com/in/justin-dekoszmovszky-5b38a91/.

Stage 16

MASTER OF THE TWO WORLDS

The Master of the Two Worlds Stage is the penultimate in the hero's journey. The hero can move seamlessly between the material everyday world and his spiritual state. Instead of being antagonistic, the hero is: "permitting the mind to know the one by virtue of the other" which "is the talent of the master," as Campbell writes.

In order to be in this place, the hero has gone through self-annihilation. Campbell illustrates this point in the following way:

> The individual, through prolonged psychological disciplines, gives up completely all attachments to his personal limitations, idiosyncrasies, hopes and fears, no longer resists the self-annihilation that is prerequisite to rebirth in the realization of truth, and so becomes ripe, at last, for the great at-one-moment. His personal ambitions being totally dissolved, he no longer tries to live but willingly relaxes to whatever may come to pass in him; he becomes, that is to say, an anonymity.[1]

DOI: 10.4324/9781032615080-17

In the initial trilogy the force acted through Luke Skywalker. Luke was a medium through which the light side of the force manifested itself, but he had not yet mastered the force. He could not really use the force to his will. In *The Last Jedi* we see Luke Skywalker sitting in a meditation position in Ahch-To and "materializing" on another planet called Crait, where he saves Rey, Leia, and the tiny rest of the resistance. In this scene he is "Master of the two Worlds" and later annihilates himself, turning into a force ghost.

Aparecida Teixeira de Morais was HR Director at Tribanco – the financial arm of Martins Group, one of Brazil's largest distributors. Part of her responsibilities for HR was training. Despite heading a corporate function, she sensed how financial literacy also influenced the success of their customers, mainly micro, small-, and medium-sized retailers. As the group's mission was to help small retailers grow, she put her skills toward service and helped to improve the financial management skills of more than 300,000 retailers all over Brazil. Her motivation, however, came from beyond business: "my heart has always led me to care about others, the common good, and the environment I'm in. It's in my DNA."[2]

You are at this stage when you have become a tool for the light side to manifest itself in business. In order to explore this stage, ask yourself: if I were the universe and would put myself (with all my skills and networks) to serve the light side – where is the best place I could put myself?

MEET YOUR JEDI MASTER: APARECIDA TEIXEIRA DE MORAIS

Aparecida Teixeira de Morais – or Cidinha, as her friends call her – studied English literature at the University of Uberlandia, Brazil. She started her professional career at Martins – a Brazilian Wholesale Company which understood that its success depends on the success of thousands of retailers, often managed by family-owners with low educational background. To support this mission, the Martins Group created a financial service institution called Tribanco in 1990. Cidinha worked her way up the ladder in the RH department, first at Martins, then at Tribanco, becoming RH Director in 2008.

As head of RH, one of her responsibilities was training of staff. Cidinha, however, recognized the power of knowledge also for clients of Tribanco and Martins Group as a whole. Her hypothesis was: if we train small retailers in financial management, we allow them to grow and foster their resilience. Following this mission, Cidinha and her team started to train small retailers in how to use credit and how to invest in the refurbishment of their stores, their stock, etc. They created Martins University for Retail – training 1,365 retailers offline and 1,833 online in 2012. Together with the International Finance Corporation they designed a module specifically for the "conscious use of credit." Aparecida started to train Tribanco's employees to become multipliers of the concept and finally took the training online. This allowed Tribanco to capacitate more than 300,000 retailers in more than 92,000 stores all over Brazil. This obviously had positive impacts on company growth, customer credit defaults, client satisfaction, and fidelity.

From a business point of view, the project helped Tribanco to establish long-term relationships with growing businesses and lower their default rate. From a human point of view, it increased the quality of life of thousands of retailers all over Brazil. In a certain sense Aparecida has turned into a force ghost by going online as it permits her idea to "materialize" in thousands of stores and screens at the same time. By combining her professional business skills with her drive to provoke social change, she won the League of Intrapreneurs global competition in 2013.[3]

Corporate Jedi Insights:

- Digitalization can be a huge leverage for impact.
- The skills of your department might be very useful in other parts of the business, such in this case training for customers.
- Did you recognize that "training" is part of many intrapreneurial projects? In the value chain of your business, who are

the people that are most in need of education? If you train them, what could be the impact on your business?

NOTES

1 Campbell, J. (1949). *The hero with a thousand faces*. Pantheon Books.

2 Grayson, D., McLaren, M., & Spitzeck, H. (2016). *Intraempreendedorismo social, jazz e outras coisas*. Alta Books.

3 See e.g. Carvalho, I. (2013, May 15). How to be a social intrapreneur: Persistence, resilience, and patience. *FastCompany*. https://www.fastcompany.com/2682063/how-to-be-a-social-intrapreneur-persistence-resilience-and-patience, as well as Grayson, D., McLaren, M., & Spitzeck, H. (2016). *Intraempreendedorismo social, jazz e outras coisas*. Alta Books.

Stage 17

FREEDOM TO LIVE

In this final stage, the hero gains his "freedom to live" because he is unafraid of death. He has made peace with his past and is not worried about his future. He gives into the nature of change. As Campbell writes: "nothing retains its own form; but Nature, the great renewer, ever makes up forms from forms. Be sure that nothing perishes in the whole universe; it does but vary and renew its form."[1] This even involves death.

Did you ever wonder: how does a Jedi die?

Remember the astonishing scene in *A New Hope* when Vader fights Obi-Wan Kenobi on the Death Star? Obi-Wan says: "if you strike me down, I shall become more powerful than you can possibly imagine." The moment Vader strikes him, his robe and lightsaber fall down, and his body has disappeared. The same happens to Luke Skywalker after the fight on Crait. Both have turned into force ghosts. Force ghosts are not fully absorbed by the Force upon death; they preserve their identity – which suggests the existence of eternal life.[2]

DOI: 10.4324/9781032615080-18

Yoda: "Eternal life . . ."
Qui-Gon Jinn: "The ultimate goal of the Sith, yet they can never achieve it; it only comes through the release of self, not the exaltation of self. It comes through compassion, not greed. Love is the answer to the darkness."[3]

The legacy of impact intrapreneurs

Let us explore legacy as a proxy of eternal life. One can distinguish four types of legacy. The first and most common is material legacy: money, monuments, constructions, artworks, etc. A second might be a natural legacy, preserved areas such as natural parks. The third form of legacy is cultural: here we see more abstract forms such as theories (e.g. relativity theory, the categorical imperative) which we pass on to future generations through education. The last and forth form of a legacy is spiritual: what do we value to such an extent that we accept sacrifices? Which values should our children adopt, e.g. love for god (religion), love for the truth (science)?

Muhammad Yunus life inspires many social entrepreneurs, as well as impact intrapreneurs. He clearly built a cultural and spiritual legacy. From a spiritual perspective one could argue that he values business as a force for good and that we should always put the human at the centre of economic activities. From a cultural point of view, he introduced the concept of "social business," an idea so powerful that it has been adopted by various organizations around the world. These ideas and values will certainly extend beyond his mortal life, making him in a certain sense "immortal."

If you reached this stage, congratulations! You completed your hero's journey. I don't want to scare you, but I have heard that some pass through various journeys during their lifetime. So, always be prepared to embark on the next adventure!

MEET YOUR JEDI MASTER: MUHAMMAD YUNUS

If you think of Corporate Jedi Masters, Muhammad Yunus might be seen as Yoda, because he is by far the wisest and most experienced. He easily uses business in favour of the common good, be it by setting up new organizations or by redirecting the purpose of existing organizations.

He was born on 28 June 1940 in the village of Bathua, Bangladesh.[4] When he participated in the matriculation exams for the Chittagong Collegiate School, he came out 16th out of 39,000 applicants. During his time at school, he joined the Boy Scouts and had the chance to travel internationally. He studied economics at Dhaka University and with the help of a Fulbright scholarship got his PhD, again in economics, from Vanderbilt University in the US. Back in Bangladesh he saw the devastating effects of the 1974 famine and became interested in poverty alleviation and started some research projects. It was in 1976 when he discovered that small loans could have a tremendous impact on poor people's lives. The idea of microcredit took form when he started to lend US $27 of his own money to 42 women in a village – each of whom were able to make a profit on the loan. Yunus was able to scale operations: in 1983 his project turned into Grameen bank (Bangladeshi for "village bank"). The Grameen Bank and Yunus received the Peace Nobel Prize in 2006 for helping to get 2 million people out of poverty. Today, even banks such as Goldman Sachs, Santander, and BNP Paribas run microcredit operations.

In the 1980s Grameen started to replicate his ideas of a social business by founding new companies such as Grameen Telecom or Grameen Software Limited next to other organizations. During the 2000s Yunus started to partner with big corporations. One of these partnerships is the Grameen-Danone joint venture, which aims to provide rural children in Bangladesh with access to key nutrients missing from their diet. By 2019, the new company had brought nutrition to more than 300,000 beneficiaries, improved the income of 500 farmers, and created more than 350 jobs.[5] To consolidate this new partnership approach, Yunus co-founded Yunus Social Business (YSB) in Germany in 2011 with the mission to "harness the power of business to end poverty and the climate crisis."[6] YSB partners with corporations such as IKEA, MAN, and SAP and has set up a dedicated programme for social intrapreneurs called "Unusual Pioneers."

For all his efforts to show that the force of business can be used for the common good, Yunus received numerous awards beyond the Peace Nobel Prize. *Fortune* magazine named him in 2012 as one of the 12 greatest entrepreneurs of the current era, stating that he "inspired countless numbers of young people to devote themselves to social causes all over the world."[7]

Corporate Jedi Insights:

- Start small: Yunus lent US $27 to a group of women and tested his model.
- Skin in the game: he invested his own money!
- Check – does it really help the beneficiaries? The women were better off and did get a chance to raise their income by using microcredits. Grameen developed serious metrics on how to measure if its beneficiaries were getting out of poverty.
- Feasibility and Scalability: do an experiment to see if your model works – Yunus saw that the women were paying back their loans. This allowed him to scale the model.
- The power of partnerships: if you find allies that share the same vision, they can help you to scale impacts – see e.g. the Grameen-Danone partnership.

WEAPON: THE THEORY OF CHANGE

Many people wonder how to measure social and/or environmental impacts of their projects. What I learnt from impact intrapreneurs is that there is no universal applicable methodology, but there is a logic to causing change. The following "theory of change" is based on the ground-breaking work of the W.K. Kellogg Foundation and its "logic model."[8] The model helps to picture how an organization defines and tracks any intended change process. Together with Simon Sinek's reflection on "Start with Why,"[9] I use the following model to help people outline their change initiative:

Let us look at an example. Peace Nobel laureate Muhammad Yunus initiated a partnership between his microcredit organization Grameen Bank in Bangladesh and Danone. I recommend you watch his very inspiring talk on YouTube called "Grameen Danone: A Social Business."[10] In Figure 17.1 you see the implicit theory of change model.

Figure 17.1 Theory of Change

Component	Key Question
Vision	Why does your project exist?
Objectives	What measurable results your project wants to achieve?
Resources & Inputs	In order to achieve your objectives, which resources and inputs do you need?
Activities	In order to achieve your objectives, which activities do you need to perform?
Output	Which are immediate results of your activities?
Outcome	Which are the qualitative changes of behaviour, knowledge, skills, development, which result from your work in a 1-3 year timeframe?
Impact	Which are the fundamental changes occurring as a result of your activities within a 7-10 year horizon?
Legacy	What has been created that will be passed to future generations?

The joint venture was started with the **vision** to improve the nutrition of children in poor rural areas in Bangladesh. By selling yoghurt fortified by micronutrients (iodine, iron, zinc, vitamin A) at very low prices, nutritional deficits of children could be relieved. This in turn leaves them healthier and less prone to miss school and in the long term fosters local development.

The measurable **objective** was to reduce the number of children in the region that presented nutritional deficits regarding the micronutrients used within the yoghurt.

To reach this objective, Grameen-Danone needed to allocate a variety of **resources**. A local factory needed to be built, milk and fruit suppliers needed to be identified, and a distribution network needed to be set up.

These resources were then put into action, executing the following **activities**: produce yoghurt, train sales ladies, measure health data, etc.

Vision	Objectives	Resources and Inputs	Activities	Outputs	Outcome	Impact	Legacy
Why does your organization exist?	What measurable results does it want to achieve?	To reach objectives, which resources and inputs are needed?	To reach objectives which activities need to be executed?	Which are immediate results?	Which qualitative changes do we expect in a 1-3 years horizon?	Which qualitative changes do we expect in a 7–10 years horizon?	What will be passed on to future generations?
Improve the nutrition of children and foster local development	Reduce the number of children which have nutritional deficits regarding Vitamin A, C and iodine.	• Yoghurt production facilities • Milk supply • Fruit supply • Distribution Channel ...	Produce yoghurt Provide logistics Sales within the community	No. of products sold No. of villages attended No. of children attended	Improvement of children´s nutrition.	Lasting improvement of children´s health indicators; School attendance rates improving; ...	It is possible to create purpose-driven businesses focussing on children´s health.

Figure 17.2 Grameen-Danone's theory of change

The first measurable result were the immediate **outputs**, such as tons of yoghurt sold, sales ladies trained, number of villages or children attended, and others.

In a second step, **outcomes** on the children's nutritional health could be evaluated. Did the deficits in terms of iron, zinc, etc. persist? Did general numbers of nutrition-related diseases decrease in the region?

In a third step and looking long-term, **impact** indicators can be tracked, such as nutritional health development of children, general children's health, absenteeism in schools, educational levels in the region, etc.

Be aware that not all projects will create a **legacy**. As the partnership between Grameen and Danone is one of the first of its kind, we might argue that the idea which might be passed to future generations is the possibility of setting up organizations, which do not depend on charity in order to address malnutrition of children. These organizations are social businesses which use business as a force for good.

CORPORATE JEDI PHILOSOPHY: YOU ARE NOT ALONE!

Impact intrapreneurs often feel alone, swimming against the corporate currents. Poe Dameron made a similar point regarding the empire in *Star Wars: Episode IX – The Rise of Skywalker*: "they win by making you think you're alone." Impact intrapreneurs see potential for impact, where others see distraction. They speak of beneficiaries instead of customers. They hear that they are the odd ones, asking questions no one ever asked before. This gives them the false impression that they are alone, that they don't belong, that there is no community of like-minded people for them. Nothing could be further from the truth.

In his foreword to our book on "Social Intrapreneurism and all that Jazz," John Elkington took us back to Apple's 1997 "Think Different" ad campaign. Its text, written by Rob Siltanen, fits perfectly to describe Corporate Jedi:

> Here's to the crazy ones. The misfits. The rebels. The troublemakers. The round pegs in the square holes. The ones who see things

> differently. They're not fond of rules. And they have no respect for the status quo. You can quote them, disagree with them, glorify or vilify them. About the only thing you can't do is ignore them. Because they change things. They push the human race forward. And while some may see them as the crazy ones, we see genius. Because the people who are crazy enough to think they can change the world, are the ones who do.[11]

Poe Dameron's quote from *The Rise of Skywalker* reads completely: "the First Order wins by making us think we're alone. We're not alone. Good people will fight if we lead them. Leia never gave up. And neither will we. We're gonna show them we're not afraid."[12]

You are not alone. John Elkington's team at SustainAbility published the first guide on impact intrapreneurs in 2008 called "The Social Intrapreneur – a Field Guide for Corporate Changemakers" showcasing intrapreneurs such as Gib Bulloch, Andreas Eggenberg, Maria Luiza Pinto, Kerryn Schrank, Luis Sota, Bob Annibale, Dan Vermeer, Bo Miller, Scott Noesen, David Berdish, Vijay Sharma, Orlando Ayala, Henry Gonzalez, Sam McCracken, Win Sakdinan, Sachin Kapila, Sue Mecklenburg, Santiago Gowland, Nick Hughes, and Susie Lonie.

The Aspen Institute launched a programme for Impact Intrapreneurs in 2009, called First Movers. As of June 2022 they have 267 fellows working in 165 companies in 22 countries. The League of Intrapreneurs counts more than 300 fellows working in 200 institutions in 27 countries. During the first five years of its existence in Brazil, FDC's Center for Intrapreneurship has identified more than 1,000 potential impact intrapreneurs, received over 200 pitches of shared value projects, accelerated 75 of those, and worked with more than 50 companies. In 2019, the Schwab Foundation for Social Entrepreneurship added Social Intrapreneurs as a new award category and identified many intrapreneurs in private companies as well as in public administration. In 2021, Yunus Social Business in collaboration with the World Economic Forum, the Schwab Foundation, and Porticus launched "Unusual Pioneers" – a programme for accelerating high level impact intrapreneurs. You are not alone – you are in very good company.

At the closing ceremony of the Inaugural League of Intrapreneurs Fellows Gathering in Paretz, Germany, Maggie De Pree lit up a candle representing the fire which nourishes impact intrapreneurs. Every one of us got a candle and we lit it at the same source, thus taking the fire of impact intrapreneurs into the whole world. There will be times when you feel alone as an impact intrapreneur. If these times come, I invite you to light a candle, feel its warmth, and watch its light – this light will connect you with all impact intrapreneurs, their joys and sorrows, their curiosity, wit, and insights, as you are part of this community. And if you need our help, we will be there for you. You may not know it, but you have millions of legions behind you!

NOTES

1 Campbell, J. (1949). *The hero with a thousand faces.* Pantheon Books.

2 "A New Hope" refers to Lucas G. (Director). (1977) *Star wars: Episode IV – a new hope* [Film], 20th Century-Fox.

3 Taken from Lucas, G. (Director). (2005). *Star wars: Episode III – revenge of the Sith* [Film]. 20th Century Fox.

4 This chapter has been constructed based on information taken from: Yunus, M. (2024). *Wikipedia.* https://en.wikipedia.org/wiki/Muhammad_Yunus; Nelson Mandela Foundation. (2024). *Muhammad Yunus: Bio.* https://www.nelsonmandela.org/content/page/muhammad-yunus-bio; Renouard, C. (2012, June 26). *A social business success story: Grameen-Danone in Bangladesh, ESSEC business school.* https://knowledge.essec.edu/en/sustainability/a-social-business-success-story.html; and Rangan, V. K., & Lee, K. (2010). *Grameen Danone Foods Ltd., a social business.* Harvard Business School Case 511-025.

5 See Boston Consulting Group and Yunus Social Business. (2013). *The power of social business.* BCG.

6 Yunus Social Business. (n.d.). *We harness the power of business to end poverty and the climate crisis.* https://www.yunussb.com/

7 Byrne, J. A. (2012, April 9). The 12 greatest entrepreneurs of our time. *Fortune.*

8 See Kellogg Foundation. (2004). *Logic model development guide.* Kellogg Foundation.

9 Sinek, S. (2009). *Start with why.* Portfolio.

10 Kubo, M. (2010, May 28). *Grameen Danone: A social business* [Video]. YouTube. https://www.youtube.com/watch?v=AV4WQV32ijs

11 Grayson, D., McLaren, M., & Spitzeck, H. (2014). *Social intrapreneurism and all that jazz.* Greenleaf.

12 Taken from Abrams, J. J. (Director). (2019). *Star wars: Episode IX – the rise of Skywalker* [Film]. Walt Disney Studios.

About the Author or Meeting My Jedi Master

On 25 January 2022 I met Master Yoda. He is quite small and many of you might remember the words he said to Luke Skywalker when they met on Dagobah: "judge me by my size, do you?"[1] I don't, as a powerful being he is. The Yoda fountain is located in the Presidio Park in San Francisco, right in front of Lucasfilm's production facilities. As the gaze of Yoda's statue caught my eye, I suddenly felt alert and my attention was drawn to my own shadow, cast by the California morning sun. In my head I could hear Yoda say: "be aware of the dark side."[1]

While there are many quotes from Yoda, two especially lead me into a deeper reflection. The first goes: "when you look at the dark side, careful you must be. For the dark side looks back."[1] My work centres around business ethics and corporate sustainability and I usually concentrate on the light side, where impact intrapreneurs create new, more sustainable business models, products, or services. I do, however, work with a lot of corporations, and many of them use sustainability as a fig leaf or even worse. In 2022, one of my Executive MBA participants was telling me that a company she worked for had set up an ethics hotline internally, in order to spot "troublemakers." Instead of using the ethics hotline for fighting immoral behaviour, they used it to spot the people with courage to speak up and fired them. "When you look at the dark side careful you must be."[1]

The second quote relates to the first and goes: "fear is the path to the dark side. Fear leads to anger. Anger leads to hate. Hate leads to suffering."[1] It would be completely understandable for people working at this organization who used the ethics hotline to fear for retaliation and feel anger for what happened to them, even to hate their previous employer. They might be tempted to turn to become a whistle-blower for the simple reason to hurt the organization, damage the reputation of the firm, and publicly blame the leadership. Again, all of this is very understandable. However, I concur with Yoda, that this would be fighting evil with evil and would ultimately lead to the dark side. I would wish for anybody who suffered from something like this to become a whistle-blower, however, with the vision to do the right thing, to improve practices and to protect others. To finish with a third quote from Master Yoda: "a Jedi uses the Force for knowledge and defense, never for attack."[1]

As you can see from this book, I prefer to look at the light side and showcase Corporate Jedi that use business as a force for good. I mean it! They intentionally use business as a tool, exploring opportunities in which impact and value-creation align. Some of you therefore might call me an optimist or criticize me for putting rose-tinted glasses on.

The stories I share aim to inspire. I believe that there are two ways to help corporations on their journey to sustainable business – the way of the doctor and the way of the master. The doctor runs a series of diagnostics, focusses on everything that is not working well, and gives you a list of unpleasant but necessary recommendations, such as drink less, do more exercise, etc. Companies do the same by hiring benchmarking exercises, comparing themselves to peers, and then recommending copying best practices, forcing new KPIs upon executives. I often see that this approach is not effective, because it does not motivate people to change. The way of the Master, however, is different. Imagine your Yoda-boss saying: you are afraid of climate change, you want to promote diversity, and you have studied at the best schools. You collected professional experiences; you know the clients and the market. I challenge you all to use your values and your knowledge and show me, how we can use this organization as a platform for change in a way that differentiates us in the market? I believe that the master approach can unlock the potential of thousands of impact intrapreneurs around the globe and accelerate our progress toward the Sustainable Development Goals. And I believe that you can be one of us!

This book is another tool I created to inspire people like you to join the impact intrapreneur movement, to use business as a force for good. If you got to this page, you've read it all. I am curious to know if it had any impact on your life and would be looking forward to any message which helps me to judge the impact of my work. You'll find me on LinkedIn and I'd be happy to hear from you. And maybe, your case will be in the next edition of this book.

May the force be with you!

NOTE

1 All Yoda quotes can be traced to: Reilly, C. (2024, January 25). 40 powerful Yoda Quotes to master your inner Jedi. *Reader´s Digest*. https://www.rd.com/article/yoda-quotes/

For Product Safety Concerns and Information please contact our EU representative GPSR@taylorandfrancis.com Taylor & Francis Verlag GmbH, Kaufingerstraße 24, 80331 München, Germany

Batch number: 10725833

Printed by Printforce, the Netherlands